"Steven Garber's collection of essays guides us in understanding the meaning of vocation and affirms our humanness; made in the very image of God, we cannot but care about the way the world is."

Philip Ng, chairman and CEO of Far East Organization

"The depth of wisdom, compelling stories, and honest questions make *The Seamless Life* a unique gift to those who seek to pursue the common good in this complex world."

Jim Mullins, coauthor of *A Symphony of Mission*

"Steven Garber's delightful prose reminds us once again of the importance of reflecting deeply upon that which is most meaningful: our very purpose. By embracing our vocation, we can each move the needle a bit from how things are to how they ought to be, showing us that we are *all* implicated in the way the world turns out."

Jay Jakub, senior director of external research, Mars, Incorporated

"*The Seamless Life* is a creative, beautiful, and winsome lens for better understanding what it is to live and love faithfully in a broken world. Steve Garber brings the rare insight that comes from years of paying close attention and listening well to the deepest longings of the human heart. This book is a gift."

Kate Harris, author of *Wonder Women: Navigating the Challenges of Motherhood, Career, and Identity*

"In *The Seamless Life*, Steven Garber culls a lifetime of observation, reflection, and writing into what can only be called a masterpiece on vocation. With gentle, persuasive, artful language, Steven gives the reader a true picture of a faithful life. It is a seamless vision of word and work based in love, lived for the benefit of all and the glory of God. I cannot recommend this manual of meaning and mission more strongly. This book contains the truest truths, the deepest wisdom, and love that knows no limits."

Charlie Peacock, Grammy Award–winning music producer

"*The Seamless Life* is a compilation of Steven Garber's serious reflections on living and loving in a wounded world. A labor of his heart, this book is a gift born of love for all of us who stumble along with him in a world hungry for shalom."

Lisa Pratt Slayton, the Tamim Partners, Pittsburgh, Pennsylvania

"One good question is better than a thousand wrong answers. *The Seamless Life* is full of good questions—excellent, profound, meaningful, surprising, deep, life-challenging, sensible questions, or simply, truthful questions. I recommend this book, hoping that you will see it as an open window, an invitation to a more seamless life."

Jozef Luptak, cellist and founder of Convergencie, Bratislava, Slovakia

"*The Seamless Life* is an accurate analysis of the crisis facing society today—a longing for wholeness. The book addresses the need for coherence between the state of our being and the act of our doing. It is unique and refreshing to read."

Eliud Wabukala, archbishop emeritus, chairman of the Ethics and Anticorruption Commission of Kenya

"Steve Garber helps us catch a glorious vision of our hope in Christ, a coherent life, a seamless life. Without denying the complexities of the already-but-not-yet world, this work enriches our perspective of the hope we have for the world to experience wholeness in various contexts: family, educational practice, economics, daily work and prayer, and many others. And *The Seamless Life* extends the compelling invitation to love and participate in God's work to heal this broken world."

Sutrisna Harjanto, president, Bandung Theological Seminary, Indonesia, and author of *The Development of Vocational Stewardship Among Indonesian Christian Professionals*

"*The Seamless Life* is at once deeply philosophical and at the same time folksy and welcoming—like Steve himself. This book is the fruit of a lifetime of work-in-love, stitched in a beautiful pattern for the pleasure our Creator and the ennobling of his readers. And this is at the heart of all his work: to please the Creator is to fully live into our own vocation."

Bruce Herman, Lothlórien Distinguished Chair in the Fine Arts, Gordon College

"In this unique book, Steven Garber gives us the chance to see the world with him, through the eyes of his mind and heart—and his deft use of a camera. These stunning photographs and written vignettes also disclose Garber's own vocation exercised in the daily struggle to see the world truthfully, to know it in its heartache and pain, and to keep loving it still. His spying heart invites us to see our own corner of the world better, honor its complicated goodness and beauty, and love our places and people with creativity, courage, and above all, hope."

Laura M. Fabrycky, author of *Keys to Bonhoeffer's Haus: Exploring the World and Wisdom of Dietrich Bonhoeffer*

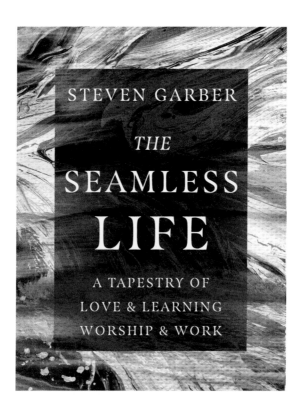

STEVEN GARBER

THE

SEAMLESS

LIFE

A TAPESTRY OF
LOVE & LEARNING
WORSHIP & WORK

ivp

An imprint of InterVarsity Press
Downers Grove, Illinois

InterVarsity Press
P.O. Box 1400, Downers Grove, IL 60515-1426
ivpress.com
email@ivpress.com

InterVarsity Press® is the book-publishing division of InterVarsity Christian Fellowship/USA®, a
movement of students and faculty active on campus at hundreds of universities, colleges, and schools
of nursing in the United States of America, and a member movement of the International Fellowship
of Evangelical Students. For information about local and regional activities, visit intervarsity.org.

All Scripture quotations, unless otherwise indicated, are taken from The Holy Bible,
New International Version®, NIV®. Copyright © 1973, 1978, 1984, 2011 by Biblica,
Inc.™ Used by permission of Zondervan. All rights reserved worldwide. www.zondervan.com.
The "NIV" and "New International Version" are trademarks registered in the United
States Patent and Trademark Office by Biblica, Inc.™

While any stories in this book are true, some names and identifying information may have been
changed to protect the privacy of individuals.

Cover design and image composite: David Fassett
Interior design: Daniel van Loon
All interior photos, unless otherwise indicated, are by Steven Garber.
Images: beach waterfront: © IakovKalinin / iStock / Getty Images Plus
  colorful paint: © photominus / iStock / Getty Images Plus
  moving water: © greenantphoto / iStock / Getty Images Plus
  textile pattern: © Sirijit Jongcharoenkulchai / EyeEm / Getty Images

ISBN 978-0-8308-4595-8 (print)
ISBN 978-0-8308-4821-8 (digital)

Printed in the United States of America ∞

InterVarsity Press is committed to ecological stewardship and to the conservation of natural resources
in all our operations. This book was printed using sustainably sourced paper.

Library of Congress Cataloging-in-Publication Data

Names: Garber, Steven, author.
Title: The seamless life : a tapestry of love and learning, worship and work / Steven Garber.
Description: Downers Grove, Illinois : IVP, an imprint of InterVarsity Press, 2020.
Identifiers: LCCN 2019041671 (print) | LCCN 2019041672 (ebook) |
  ISBN 9780830845958 (print) | ISBN 9780830848218 (digital)
Subjects: LCSH: Christian life.
Classification: LCC BV4501.3 .G369 2020 (print) | LCC BV4501.3 (ebook) | DDC 248.4—dc23
LC record available at https://lccn.loc.gov/2019041671
LC ebook record available at https://lccn.loc.gov/2019041672

P 25 24 23 22 21 20 19 18 17 16 15 14 13 12 11 10 9 8 7 6 5 4 3 2 1
Y 37 36 35 34 33 32 31 30 29 28 27 26 25 24 23 22 21 20

CONTENTS

For my grandchildren,
longing that you will live into the vision of a seamless life,
a coherence between who you are and why you are,
giving meaning to what you do with the lives that are yours.

A BEGINNING

MOST OF LIFE is pretty autobiographical.

We are sons of Adam and daughters of Eve, each one with histories written into the history of people who have lived through the centuries and cultures before us, the joys and sorrows of their lives mysteriously twined into the very meaning of our lives. It cannot not be.

True for everyone everywhere, it is true of me.

Almost always, when someone asks, "Why do you think about vocation like you do?" I will simply say that it begins with my Grandfather Gilchrist, and tell the tale of the way that *ora et labora*, prayer and work, were woven into the meaning of his life. That he allowed me in—summer after summer, year after year, giving me the gift of seeing over his shoulder and through his heart as he prayed and worked—has formed me, heart and mind, soul and strength.

My grandparents lived between Durango and Cortez, Colorado, in the grand geography known as the Four Corners—the wonderful place in the American Southwest where the mesas meet the mountains. It is a land that I still love. My earliest memories are of its air and the wonder of the wind blowing through the aspen leaves, gracing its meadows and river valleys, making the world new again, morning by morning. At least, it seemed that way to me as a child. They had cattle, and I gloried in them, from my first years knowing the differences between the breeds and why they mattered. I still remember an exceptional morning walking through the corral by the barn, a very little boy that I was, and meeting an Angus bull who began to chase me. I thought I was going to die.

There were better days though, many of them. Riding horseback through the pastures, catching frogs in creeks and bringing them home for my always-and-ever kind grandmother who fried their legs. And then best of all, rounding up my relatives for a home-grown rodeo, complete with calves who bucked their best.

One day a Navajo man came to the ranch, asking if my grandfather would trade a blanket for a cow. They made a deal, and through the years of my boyhood the blanket was my grandfather's saddle blanket; not a collector's item, but a simple, ordinary saddle blanket, bearing the smells and sweat of a horse. When my grandfather died, the blanket became mine, and over many years I have prized it, loving what it means to me about the life and world that is mine to remember.

The blanket now graces a shelf full of books that matter to me, all on the theme of vocation, the complex and rich word that it is. As this book was being born, one morning I laid the blanket out on the floor of Regent College's art gallery, and then walked around it, wanting to get the light and shadow right, hoping that I could find a way to capture its native beauty and textured meaning—its history threading its way through the years of my life, a memory for me of what seamlessness is and ought to be.

This is a book about vocation, but a different book, a collection of essays and photos. An unusual effort for the publisher, it is new for me too. Rather than making an argument that is developed over scores of pages and many chapters, this one is a deeper and deeper reflection on one question: *What does it mean to see seamlessly?* To see the whole of life as important to God, to us, and to the world—the deepest and truest meaning of vocation—is to understand that our longing for coherence is born of our truest humanity, a calling into the reality that being human and being holy are one and the same life.

Yes, *ora et labora*, in my life and in yours.

Photo of my grandfather's saddle blanket.

MADISON AVENUE, MAD
MEN, AND MUCH MORE

MADISON AVENUE. Mad Men. Image and reality. True stories and sort-of-true stories and not-so-true stories.

While visiting New York City, very close to Madison Ave., I thought about the stories of our lives. Where do they come from? Who tells them? Should we believe them?

Having watched most of *Mad Men*—falling, falling, falling as they do—I was intrigued by another story, this one of a company called FiveStone, which offers a different way to imagine the meaning of the marketplace. As their website says, "FiveStone locks arms with organizations fighting to make the world a better place. We use design to help nonprofits and social enterprises solve their biggest challenges and create positive impact.... We want to see a world where thoughtful organizations win and good pushes itself into every aspect of society."

Brought into being by Jason Locy, a Virginian now living in Brooklyn, his company tells stories about ideas, about organizations, about businesses, doing their best to tell the truth about the way things are in a way that is imaginative, compelling, and engaging. Not spinning but instead listening carefully and then creatively offering windows into what honestly is, even as every one of us dreams of what might be—doing something that is rare but is at the heart of the best stories, always.

The day before I got there, Jason was in Detroit at work for a client whose work is to bring renewal to debilitated schools. Nothing very romantic about that, but seeing his labor as written into the calling to seek the flourishing of the city—wherever the city may be found—he has drawn his team of creatives around what the schools are doing, what still needs to be done, and what help they need to accomplish their vision.

One shelf in their office is devoted to Tegu Blocks, another client, whose hard work and global vision have brought into the marketplace a toy that children love. All kinds of creative play are possible with a little help from a magnet built into the colored blocks of every different shape. Their website tells their tale: "We believe that every child possesses the ability to build, create, and imagine. Tegu blocks are a canvas for their imagination. No instruction manuals or electronics, just toys that inspire limitless creativity across all ages."

The day before I was with the leadership of the Praxis Labs, another client of FiveStone, whose own remarkable vision and creativity are drawing together entrepreneurs from all over the world who want their labors to both do well and do good. And some will know of the work of Q, the yearly and more gathering of people in the cities of America to think about and work on complex questions at the heart of our common good; they too are a client of FiveStone.

Watching *Mad Men* as I have over the last few years, seeing Donald Draper fall and fall and fall some more, seeing how hard it is to imagine the life and work of Madison Avenue to be anything other than Spin (with a capital S), it was a grace to enter into another way to be human, seeing that it is possible to live and work and have one's being right in the middle of Manhattan and at the end of the day still stand with one's integrity intact—knowing that all of us have flourished more fully because of their good work.

Photo from the streets of New York.

ON GOOD BUSINESS

CAN BUSINESS EVER BE JUST ABOUT BUSINESS? Or politics just about politics? Or the arts just about the arts? Or education just about education?

The wisest wisdom has always said no.

Life is too complex for all of us. One area of life is connected to every other area of life—by the very nature of the universe (*uni*-verse that it is)—which is why the most important learning we do is interdisciplinary, the in-between conversations that connect the conversations the disciplines have on their own. To master cellular biology is not the same thing as mastering nineteenth-century English literature; the questions of the one are not the questions of the other. So it is not that specialization is an evil; there are times when we want someone who has spent the years required to understand the precise character of the brain, its intricacies, its dimensions, its diseases and pathologies—and of course what is needed to repair it.

But even brain surgeons need to be human beings too, first and last. They need to be intelligent, but in a multidimensional way—and so morally intelligent, emotionally intelligent, historically intelligent, sociologically intelligent, and more—if their gifts are to honestly serve the common good.

I thought of this on the day I spent several hours at the Mars corporation headquarters, taking part in a serious conversation about economics and the world, particularly about the way business ought to be done if human beings are to flourish.

For several years I have been working with Mars on the *economics of mutuality*, a morally and institutionally serious effort to rethink the very way business works in the world. For a many-billion-dollar-a-year company to even ask that question is unusual, perhaps rare. In fact, why even bother? Isn't business, business? And if you can make enough money to be charitable at the end of the year, isn't that all that can be expected? Maybe even more than can be expected?

But what if justice and mercy, honesty and integrity, truthfulness from beginning to end were the contours of our lives and labors? What if we decided that good business necessarily requires a more complex bottom line, a rethinking of the very purposes of business? What if doing well and doing good were a seamless reality? What if personal convictions were integrally woven into public practices? And of course, in the middle of our conversation was the hard work of making peace with the proximate—of something that is right and good and true and just, even if we cannot find our way to everything, where every wrong is righted and every hope is addressed finally and fully.

We were hosted by Jay Jakub, the director of external research at Mars, and long a friend, the one who initially drew me in to this work. Jay is one of the two executives who lead this project at Mars and are the coauthors of *Completing Capitalism* in which they set forth their thesis and hope. Two friends who lead other organizations joined in, Michael Bontrager, CEO of the Chatham Financial Corporation, and Mark Rodgers, principal of the Clapham Group, who brought their own commitments and insights into the conversation. To a person, we have given years to careful and critical evaluation of the marketplaces of the world: working in the global financial markets as Michael does, and consulting with the largest foundations in the world as Mark does, and then me too, in my own "always the professor at the table" in the conversations of my world. As Jay put it, "You are the one who reminds us of purpose, of why we are doing this and what this is about." I hope so.

For most of my life I have been drawn to people who ask hard questions. Or at least questions that question the status quo, the way it's "always been done." Perhaps it was coming of age in the counterculture or being a second son or maybe even my deepest instincts formed by my faith in the counterreality of the kingdom of God being the primary reality, but from the first days when I was beginning to grow beyond my childhood beliefs about everything, I have yearned for something more. The connections between things have mattered to me—if this is true, then what about this? and how does this relate to that?

The people I am drawn to are like that too, in their very-different-from-me ways. I will never be an executive for a global corporation, a CEO of another, a political strategist either, or anyone but frail, finite me—but to have friends who long for coherence across the whole of life is a gift; each one bringing unique but collaborative vocations to bear on our common calling, each one asking deeper questions about coherence, about the interrelationships of ideas and beliefs, of practices and choices, not only for individuals but for institutions as well.

Years ago I was persuaded that the "nothing-but" approach to life was flawed. That human beings are "nothing but." That sex is nothing but. That work is nothing but. That psychology is nothing but. That politics is nothing but.

Yet everything is more than that because everyone is more than that. Our conversation, in the midst of the Mars corporation and its M&Ms, was a signpost that pointed to a different way, arguing against the belief that "business is nothing but." Simply said, it was a reminder that sometimes in some places some people give their very lives for something more.

Photo taken at the Mars corporation in McLean, Virginia.

REPAIRING THE WORLD

THERE ARE TIMES WHEN I FEEL LIKE I am walking through the day trying to repair the world. One morning I put on worn-out jeans and painted in my son David's house in Anacostia, for too long a forgotten part of the city of Washington. After some years of dreaming and working in that neighborhood, he was selling his house. It was a horrible mess when he bought it, completely full of junk and garbage everywhere, and he slowly made it new, renovating it from top to bottom. He hoped to put it on the market quickly, and so he had been working on it, getting it ready, and I wanted to help.

I had planned to come home, get cleaned up, and then go to my afternoon meeting at the headquarters of a global corporation that I consult with. But painting "one last section" kept me longer, and I decided to just go as is. It was okay because we met offsite in a restaurant that didn't mind.

This company makes things that people all over the world enjoy, by the billions of dollars' worth. For years now I have worked with them on rethinking the way that business is done, in fact the way that economic life is ordered, and as the months pass, that work only becomes more intriguing and complex. Some time ago I offered my colleagues there the vision of *tikkun olam*, a long-ago Hebrew way of describing our vocation as human beings to "repair the world," seeing ourselves as responsible for the way things turn out. For years I have been intrigued by what this image means and what it assumes.

Most of us see the sorrows and horrors of life, and groan. Things are not the way they are supposed to be. But the language of "supposed to be" makes assumptions about the very meaning of life. There are really only a few ways of seeing life that can make sense of "supposed to be." Not all ideas are equal; they just can't be. Not all stories tell the same story; how could they?

For example, drawing on the analysis of my favorite philosopher-poet—Bono of U2, who sees karma written into most ways of making sense of life and the world, whether the materialism of the West ("I am my DNA, and therefore the wiring has already been done and I have no responsibility"), or the pantheism of the East ("The fates have already decided what is and will be, and therefore I have no responsibility")—without grace we are stuck, metaphysically and morally, in moments we cannot get out of. And that's a problem.

To speak of repairing the world assumes that we see some things as wrong. But if what *is* is right, then what is wrong? Nothing, really. Personal preference matters, but not very much. At the end of the day, what I like bumps up against what you like—and "it is what it is." Whether a broken house or a broken economy, things are as they are. After all, what *is* is right.

But human beings that we are, there is something in us that cries out. We do groan. We do sigh. We do protest. And sometimes, we long for something more, maybe even for the way "things are supposed to be."

Yet we are reminded that every effort at repairing the world costs us. We will get hurt because it is very messy, and never neat and clean. To take up the wounds of the world will wound us.

This week I went "further up and further in" (remembering the allusive wisdom of Aslan in C. S. Lewis's *The Last Battle*) to the vocation of *tikkun olam*, a calling that belongs to all of us, wherever we are in the world. The vision makes sense of the brokenness of life, of everyone's life, of life for everyone, whether my son's house or my colleagues' business, or the heartaches of neighbors a world away. We yearn for things to be made right, for life to be as it could be, as it might be, as it should be—as it is supposed to be.

Photo taken at my son's house in the Anacostia neighborhood of Washington, DC.

SEEK THE FLOURISHING
OF THE CITY

NONE OF US can care for everything everywhere. So we choose to care about something somewhere.

I thought of that while getting to know two men who have chosen a people and a place near the Rift Valley in Kenya. As they set out their vision for a work that is a mile deep and an inch wide, I was surprised at the richness and texture of their commitment to the little place of Maai Mahiu—developing programs in education, environment, economy, health, and community—realizing that most of the time most of us have a hard time settling in like that. We know so much in the media-driven information age that to choose, for love's sake, to become responsible for one people in one place is very unusual. But they have, and they intend to keep at it.

We spent hours together at the Praxis Labs in the Catskills of New York, about an hour-and-a-half north of New York City. These two men were chosen to take part in a year-long cohort of entrepreneurs giving heart and soul to seeing their dreams become reality. The more I listened, the more intrigued I was at the way discipline and affection were twined together.

"After living in Kenya my first year in 2000, I started to recognize that we could not address one area of need adequately without addressing all areas equally," explains founder Zane Wilemon. "Why? Because they're all connected. Deforestation leads to poor water supply. Poor water supply leads to economic deficiency. Economic deficiency leads to lack of health care and education . . . and the cycle continues."

Zane is a Texan and lives some of the year in Austin. As a twenty-two-year-old he bought a one-way ticket to Kenya and taught for a year in the Rift Valley Academy, learning much about God, himself, and the world. But that year he also met Jeremiah Kuria, whose family had long lived in this part of Kenya. They began having lunch together every week, hearing each other's lives, beginning to imagine a life together.

One of the most fascinating parts of the story is that in their efforts to seek the flourishing of their city, Zane decided to pursue Whole Foods, which is headquartered in Austin, to see what might be done together on behalf of Africa. He tried and tried and tried, with remarkable creativity and persistence joined together with his holy Texas swagger—and it worked. Finally, it worked! The result has been a business relationship between the women of Maai Mahiu and Whole Foods, the stores selling products produced by the women. There is more to tell someday.

But as we sat in our Adirondack chairs while Zane recounted this journey, I found myself thinking about the prophet Jeremiah and his searching words of vocation for the exiled people of Israel now living in Babylon. "Seek the flourishing of the city. Build houses. Plant trees. Get married. Have children. Pray for the city, understanding that when it flourishes, you will flourish." And I smiled, seeing a twenty-first-century Jeremiah sitting beside me, knowing that he was working this out in his own place among his own people.

Visions of vocation have to become flesh. They have to be worked out and lived into among friends, in neighborhoods, in small towns and big cities, and sometimes even in places like Austin and Maai Mahiu, and Babylon.

Photo taken at the Praxis Labs in the Adirondacks, New York.

THE WAY THE WORLD
IS SUPPOSED TO BE

THE WAY THE WORLD'S SUPPOSED TO BE.

Is there a world like that? Do we know? How would we? What does it mean? These are the greatest questions of life, ones that we answer very differently given our deepest commitments about the meaning of life, our beliefs about God, the human condition, and history.

For some, it is a clear no, sure as we are that no one knows and no one can, so it is arrogance to assume that we know anything like that. Others aren't quite sure, so rather than weighing in with confidence on one side or the other, they simply step away from any presumed certainty. And others hope so, sure that something is true because everything cannot be "whatever," that justice cannot be "just us."

None of this can remain in the abstract for long.

Some time ago I was with the Pittsburgh Leadership Foundation, looking out on the city from Station Square. For a day, they convened a group of people with long commitments to Pittsburgh, going further up and further in, to PLF's decades-long engagement of the most difficult questions and concerns of the city. In the language of the prophet Jeremiah, they have longed for "the flourishing of the city" and have kept at that for years, taking up Pittsburgh's hopes and fears with new and renewed energy through generations. For that reason alone, their work is remarkable.

I was asked to finish the day, reflecting on what I had heard and what it meant. Like all cities, Pittsburgh is a story-shaped community, one that runs across the centuries. The history is long and complex, but I chose to begin by remembering Robert Lavelle, the Hill District banker whose work long served the financially underserved of Pittsburgh, and Sam Shoemaker, the Episcopal rector who spent years praying for Pittsburgh to become "as well-known for God as it was for steel," telling about their contributions to the story of the city. And after rooting this in the vision of jubilee, a window into the way the world's supposed to be—which happens to be the name of a conference hosted in Pittsburgh for the past forty years—I drew into the conversation the vision of Wendell Berry, not from Pittsburgh but a man who writes for all of us.

In his essay "Two Economies," Berry argues that everywhere we look, there are "lesser economies." For example, the University of Pittsburgh Medical Center, Pittsburgh itself, the state of Pennsylvania, and finally the United States each in their own ways are lesser economies, creating and managing metrics that judge their effectiveness and profitability over the course of time. But he then argues that there is a "greater economy" too, one that we don't get to decide, to choose, to prefer, or to want because it is the world that is really there, whether we believe in it or not. Sometimes described as "the most serious essayist in America today," Berry simply says that the greater economy is "the kingdom of God." "You can call it what you want to call it," says Berry, but we do not get to deny it.

And over the pages of his essay he maintains that the lesser economies must eventually live within the reality of the greater economy. That will happen because their limited, or lesser, visions of economic well-being—the commonweal, or commonwealth (good word that is for the "commonwealth of Pennsylvania")—will finally be judged by reality, by the world that is really there.

The implications cross the whole of life, of course, far beyond their meaning for economies. From sexuality to marriage, from local politics to international diplomacy, we choose, able to respond as we are, responsible as we are. And our choices have consequences, for blessing and curse. At the end of the day, though, our pretensions and imaginations are constrained by the contours of the cosmos because, after all, reality is reality.

Because this was Pittsburgh, it was impossible not to think about the history of the city, the Steel City it was and no longer is, which is a strange, surprising historical unfolding of Shoemaker's prayer. Books have been written, dissertations have been defended, and of course thousands of lives have been lived through the complexity of this history, and there is of course a longer, deeper story. But this is true: the failure to see the lesser economy as necessarily written into the meaning of the greater economy brought about the implosion of the steel industry. To put it simply: robber barons cannot keep robbing and unions cannot keep unionizing, each seeing their respective interest as a zero-sum game. When each chose to strangle the other, everyone lost. Steel is still being made, but not in Pittsburgh.

I talked about my work with the Mars corporation and its unusual vision of "an economics of mutuality," a surprisingly serious effort to rethink the purpose of business by creating metrics that account for a more complex bottom line. If it is long-term profitability that we care about, making money over the long haul, then the more complex bottom line is almost pure *realeconomik*, the reality of economics formed by the reality of the greater economy. Not corporate social responsibility and not green spin, the economics of mutuality is a fundamental reworking of the very nature of our commonwealth, one that honestly accounts for profit, for people, and for the planet—not privileging one as "the real bottom line" but honestly accounting for all three as integral to a healthy business and economy, for sustained profitability.

More was said that day with the Pittsburgh Leadership Foundation, but what was good about that day was that there were serious people in the room who have long loved their city and who are asking the most important questions about what its flourishing will require of them. Born of a shared vision of vocation, they are giving themselves to being common grace for the common good, hoping their work in Pittsburgh is a signpost for the way the world could be and someday will be.

Photo from Mount Washington looking down onto Pittsburgh, Pennsylvania.

A CONVERSATION
ABOUT CALLING

SOMETIMES HEAVEN MEETS EARTH in a hamburger.

At least I think that's possible—and when we try, working hard to figure out why food that is tasty and healthy at the same time matters, it becomes almost sacramental. Over lunch at Elevation

Burger, home to "burgers the way they're meant to be," heaven and earth, hamburgers and why ingredients matter, and the sacramental life (and even the good music of U2) were woven together into the conversation.

A young man from Charlottesville, Virginia, had driven up to Washington, DC, to talk about his life. After some years on the road as a musician, his band's music ringing its way up the staircase of fame, he was beginning to think through what he wanted to do with the rest of life. But that brings up all sorts of things, some clear and some not so clear. As we have talked about vocations and the arts over the years, about the meaning of music for life and the world, he wondered what I might think.

Of course, that didn't matter nearly as much as what he was thinking about the future, of what he wanted to do and why. The words *vocation* and *occupation* more often than not thread their way through my conversations, and I do my best to make clear that there is a difference and why the difference is important. The one is a word about the deepest things, the longest truths about each of us: what we care about, what motivates us, why we get up in the morning. The other is a word about what we do day by day, *occupying* particular responsibilities and relationships along the way as we live into our vocations. They aren't the same word, and understanding that matters.

So I wanted to hear what he was thinking, and not surprisingly, given who he is—a remarkably thoughtful, serious, kind, humble person—he was thinking things through with characteristic care, sifting and weighing things that matter most: his young marriage, his gifts and interests, where he lives, and the community that is his. He sees himself situated and wants to make decisions that honor those commitments.

Along the way the words *seamless* and *coherence* came up, and we talked about them in relation to his life. He understood what I meant, and responded by saying, "I was born into that way of seeing; my education at Rivendell School was that. We were taught to think seamlessly."

Yes, Rivendell, such a place it was and is—for hobbits wherever they may be found. I confess that I smiled, probably even more deeply in my heart than he could see on my face. My wife, Meg, and I were involved at Rivendell for many years. Along with others, Meg spent a lot of time writing curriculum for its first years, offering an almost unique vision of learning for those with eyes to see. In a word, it was seamless, a curricular vision that did its best to bring all of life, all of learning, into a coherent whole, unit by unit. So whether studying animals, Virginia, oceans, the Civil War, or the Reformation, Meg imaginatively created ways to learn to read the best stories and learn to spell at the same time, to make sense of history and to understand geography at the same time, to count numbers and to develop scientific skills at the same time.

This young man understood this in the deepest, truest sense as he reflected back on the last years of his life, seeing his music written into his vocation, even as he began to wonder what will be the next occupation that will take him further up and further in to who he is and what he cares about.

We ate well, even if simply. Tasty and healthy at the same time, and so a signpost of meals to come—almost sacramental, I suppose. His life will be his, but as he steps into the future, I hope he will see in the coherence of his calling and career a way for heaven and earth to meet, sometimes in some places. At our best, at our truest, I think we all want that.

Photo from Elevation Burger in Falls Church, Virginia.

WORK MATTERS

FOR ALL THAT THE MARXIST-LENINIST VISION got badly wrong, they got this right: work matters.

And work matters because it has social meaning, even political meaning, especially economic meaning, and most importantly, transcendent meaning. Even if they got its meaning wrong, tragically wrong, they saw something that was true. Captured in their iconic symbol of the sickle and hammer, always and everywhere it is an argument that the ordinary work of ordinary human beings is at the heart of history.

Several years ago I saw this on the streets of Kerala in the southwest corner of India. Still, the only honestly elected communist government in the world, the banners over every avenue are an ongoing debate between Marx and Mao: Who is right? Who is more right? What is not in question is their belief that if the workers of the world unite, the world will be a better place. What is not in question is their conviction that work matters.

I have often wondered why we in the West have so often missed that. Johnny Paycheck crooning "Take this job and shove it—I ain't working here no more!" was one particularly painful window into that reality, but it is a story we keep telling because it is a reality we keep experiencing. In their different ways, the films *Modern Times, The Man in the Gray Flannel Suit, Ikuru, The Graduate, Reality Bites, Wall Street, 9 to 5, El Norte, The Devil Wears Prada,* and *Up in the Air* tell the same tale from very different places in the socioeconomic spectrum across our history of filmmaking. But we can pick our moment and our artistic expression of the human longing for work to be more, to mean more than just a job, because we all long for something more.

With industrial capitalism has come glory and shame. Flourishing of all sorts, yes, but heartache for so many too. On the one hand, who among us looks the gift horse in the mouth? Dental care, abundant food, heart surgery, planes, trains, and automobiles, and so much more. And yet, and yet, on the other hand, not everyone has the same access. Some in fact are actually alienated; remember Pittsburgh's steelworkers or Detroit's carmakers—Marx got that part right.

Charles Dickens saw this 150 years ago. Think about Ebenezer Scrooge and Tiny Tim. Isn't our very favorite tale of Christmas about the cracks in capitalism, circa 1850? Of those who had and those had not? Of those who had figured out how to use the system and those who suffered because of the system? Sometimes it seems strange that we love Dickens and despise Marx; both men were writing about the same things in the same city in the same years. One told stories we still love, and the other protested so passionately that radical revolutions the world over changed the next century.

In the end Marx and his followers, the Lenins, the Trotskys, the Stalins, the Maos, the Castros, brought untold sorrow to human beings wherever his protest was heard—socially, politically, and economically. The root of his flawed vision was his misreading the meaning of work: it could never save, and it was never going to have the transcendent meaning Marx gave to it.

But work is bursting with meaning if we have eyes to see what it is and what it isn't. And labor is written into the meaning of life if we have eyes to see it as integral, not incidental, to the *missio Dei*.

I think about these things. And I thought of all this again when I visited the Grohmann Museum in Milwaukee. In a word, it was amazing. Imagined and funded by a local industrialist, Eckhart Grohmann, the museum is completely focused on "Man at Work" and is a celebration of human labor. Work of all kinds is honored and remembered in beautiful paintings and sculpture: the earliest stories we know about human life and labor under the sun, the most modern forms of industrial capitalism that we have imagined, medieval merchants and physicians as well, with men and women at work in the fields of the world, and a bronze cowboy by Remington too. And on and on and on.

Why work? The Grohmann answers the question artfully. With its commitment to the meaning of good work, even of heartbreaking work, sometimes even of backbreaking work, the stories its art tells allow every one of us to reflect on who we are and what we do, standing on the shoulders of our fathers and mothers over the centuries who have spent the days of their lives at work in the world. The best art always allows us to come in, to see something of ourselves, to know something about ourselves that we would not be able to see or know otherwise.

One more time, Walker Percy was right: bad books always lie; they lie most of all about the human condition. And bad art of every kind always lies, missing the meaning of who we are—just as good art tells the truth about the human condition. The Grohmann honors us as the glorious ruins we are. Created to work, we are to find meaning in our work. But also we are able to distort the meaning of our work, imagining that our work means more or less than it ought.

Getting it right matters because work matters.

Photo of statue at the rooftop gallery of Grohmann Museum in Milwaukee, Wisconsin.

CULT. CULTIVATE.
CULTURE.

WORDS MATTER.

A few years ago in Bratislava, Slovakia, at the conference "Visions for the Marketplace," in one lecture I talked about three words: *cult*, *cultivate*, *culture*. They are not only etymologically connected but philosophically too. They define each other, each in its own way growing out of the other. They push and shove each other, moving back-and-forth on each other, twining themselves in and around each other. But what do they mean in relation to each other? And why does it matter?

Several years ago Meg and I were in Switzerland visiting our daughter, Eden, who was working in a small village within a community called L'Abri, a French word for "the shelter." For three generations now the residents of L'Abri have opened their hearts and homes to young people with honest questions wanting honest answers. When I was twenty, I hitchhiked my way there. And in my daughter's day, after a semester of study in Geneva, Switzerland, she too found her way up the mountainside with her own hopes. Several years later it had become a second home, and in her last days there, wanting to see and hear something of her experience, we visited; I even was asked to give a lecture, which seemed a wonderful if unexpected experience to me after all those years.

One day I saw a sign on the door of the French-speaking Protestant church in Huémoz, the Swiss village that is home to L'Abri, simply saying that "the cult is meeting down the mountain this week." My first instinct was to groan, wondering what had happened! And then I realized that in French, like in all Romance languages, *cult* was not a pejorative word as it is in English. But what did it mean? And what did it mean in relation to *culture*, which is a word I think a lot about? Not long after, I began searching the etymological dictionaries of the world, wondering what the words mean and where they had come from. What intrigued me was that both *cult* and *culture* grew out of *cultivation*, which is the oldest of the three words.

Given that I have long believed that for everyone everywhere the first human vocation was to cultivate the created order, to see what is possible to be done on the face of the earth, I began to ponder what *cult* and *culture* mean in relationship to *cultivation*. I concluded that for all of us—whatever we believe about the deepest things—the most important things about life and the world are "cultic" by definition. We are, after all, *homo adorans* because we will make something or someone most important, and so we will worship, we will love, we will adore. There are no exceptions. Buddhists will. Maoists will. Evolutionary materialists will. Jews will. Muslims will. Christians will. As Augustine said so perceptively, the question "What do you love?" is the deepest of all questions, probing us in our heart of hearts, seeing into the truest motive of our motivations.

In our different ways, we all believe in something, holding it uncritically because our deepest beliefs must be believed uncritically. We all have pretheoretic commitments about reality that affect what we see and why we see what we see. The uncritically held belief that some are just neutral because they are "not religious" is a fantasy. As the great scientist Michael Polanyi wrote with unusual honesty and insight, "The viewer is always viewing." We see out of our hearts because we see out of our pretheoretic commitments. No one is neutral.

And so from our cultic commitments we live and move and have our being, cultivating life and the world. Can you grow grapes and then make wine? A guitar from this wood? A house from these stones? A city from these houses? And on and on, all the way to U2 concerts, Hong Kong, MRIs, and iPhones. The most interesting questions, the most important questions always are: Who or what is our reason for being? Why do we do the things we do? What does it all mean?

Our vocations grow out of our beliefs about the way things are, about what matters and what doesn't matter; what we do with life is born out of our commitments about the meaning of life. Habits of heart that form common practices are born of ways of life that come from deeply held commitments about the most important things, and this reality has a thousand faces.

The culture of California is different from the culture of Montana is different from the culture of Texas is different from the culture of Minnesota is different from the culture of Virginia is different from the culture of Maine. Pittsburgh has a different culture from New Orleans and different again from Denver. The culture of Prague is different from the culture of Bratislava is different from the culture of Vienna, just as the culture of London is different from the cultures of Dublin and Paris.

But we also speak of a Hindu culture just as we speak of a Jewish culture just as we speak of a materialist culture. This is as true across human hearts and history and so is true of the most ardent secularists as it is of the most devout theists.

So in the gathering in Bratislava, speaking to morally serious people who long to understand more fully their own responsibility for the ways of life in Central Europe—everyone in their own way hungry for vocations that contribute to healthier social ecologies—I offered them the vision of vocation born of the cult-cultivate-culture dynamic. It is rich and complex, with consequences that run across the whole of life. Human flourishing is at stake, and that was plainly the conviction of those who imagined the conference. They are giving their lives for the sake of human flourishing, being common grace for the common good, believing that their Christian faith implicates them in that complex vocation, for love's sake seeing themselves responsible for Bratislava, for Slovakia, for Central Europe, and for the world.

On the way home from Bratislava, I spent a day in Vienna, and saw this sign on the door of an Orthodox Jewish synagogue:

Israelitische Kultusgemeinde Wien. It translates, "Vienna Israelite Community." The German word *Kultus* is written into the name. From their deepest commitments about life and reality, for hundreds of years they have come together to form a common life, living from those beliefs in the day by day of time and place, and over generations a *culture* has been created.

Cult. Cultivate. Culture. And back again. The words play themselves out, affecting and shaping each other, always and everywhere. It cannot not be.

Photo from a Jewish synagogue in Vienna, Austria.

A TERRIBLE BEAUTY

INTRACTABLE.

It is a hard word, and one we wish wasn't. Whenever we find ourselves needing that word, we are in a miserable place. Sometimes marriages seem like that, and we can see no way other than more sorrow. And sometimes work bring us into messes that we groan over, knowing that there is only more mess ahead. Then sometimes the issues are more social and political, even global—ones that pit people against people, histories against histories, hopes against hopes.

Yes, *intractable* is the word.

And I have heard that word too many times, but it is an honest word for the perennial tensions between the Israeli and Palestinian peoples. Convened by the visionary and courageous people who call themselves Telos, brought into being by the commitments and callings of Todd Deatherage and Gregory Khalil, several hundred people met at the United States Institute of Peace, a beautifully imagined building rightly situated in a geographical triangle with the State Department and the Lincoln Memorial. With State being the guardian of our national interests around the world, and the Memorial remembering "with malice towards none, with charity for all" for the ages, the Institute was the right place for Telos to bring together men and women who long for a conversation with consequences.

There wasn't a cheap word all day because there couldn't be. We felt the weight of the world as speaker after speaker offered analysis and insight, argument and judgment, necessarily sober—*intractable* was the word, after all—but always with hope, born of belief in the truest truths of the universe, as hard as that is to see in our through-a-glass-darkly lives. Jews spoke, as did Muslims, and so did Christians, but then so did secularists, each one there for a common "telos," everyone longing for the peace of Jerusalem.

As I looked around the room, I could see people from the marketplaces of the world, as well as the churches, synagogues, and mosques. But there were others who came from positions in governments and universities, still others represented the right-of-center political vision and others the left-of-center, each with some true passion for another way forward than the eye-for-an-eye real-politik that shapes our current reading of what is and what can be. Ambassadors spoke with seasoned wisdom, but activists did too, filled-to-the-brim with their yearning to disrupt the status quo.

The longer I watched, the more I thought about a film I had seen. It had nothing to do with Jerusalem and the children of Abraham. In fact it was almost a million miles from that place and that people. An Australian movie based on a true story of tribes who live on a small island in the South Pacific who have spent centuries at war with each other, generation after generation killing and being killed, *Tanna* tells the tale of a girl who wants to marry the man she wants to marry, almost a Romeo and Juliet among Aboriginal people. But traditions that seem written into the stone of their civilization make that impossible, and the young couple find themselves in an intractable situation. There is love, yes, but there is hate too. At a critical moment another way is offered, one that requires an unusual grace, a seemingly impossible grace—but someone would have to say no to the tribalism that has terrorized their common life, and that is the dramatic tension of the film.

The story of those people in that place is not very far from those who call the Holy Land home. What is true in the South Pacific is true in the Middle East; we are perennial people, after all. Zero-sum games never make for honest winners—either in marriages or in the rest of life—because someone must lose. But this is precisely why the calculus at the heart of the Telos project argues that there are two honest histories and two honest hopes in Israel, and therefore both must be honestly honored. It is a short-term political fiction to imagine otherwise.

Before the day was done, we had artists join us too. Remarkably gifted and wonderfully skilled, the musicians who call themselves

The Brilliance brought their rich, evocative, haunting melodies that carry the deepest, truest poetry that is being sung today. Right in the middle of the evening was the novelist Colum McCann who lyrically and beautifully reflected on why stories matter for human flourishing, whether in the age-old conflict in his native Ireland or the tension-of-the-day, the Israel-Palestinian mess. We could have listened longer to the songs and the stories, as they carried our hearts to hopes beyond what seems to all honest eyes, simply, sadly, *intractable*.

In his eloquent, passionate address, McCann offered the image of the work of Telos as "a terrible beauty," a painful image but quite profound, born of a vocation that refuses to romanticize, but also that refuses to give into the cynicism that things that are, must be. To work for a future that is a signpost of what should be is hard work—but every other alternative is worse.

Photo of Todd Deatherage of Telos at the United States Institute of Peace in Washington, DC.

LEARNING ABOUT
VOCATION

"Mamas, don't let your babies grow up to be cowboys."
So sang Willie Nelson, and I never believed it to be true. Simply
said, I am my grandfather's grandson, and he was a hero to me for
all the days of my life. I can still see him ride off on his horse in the
morning, spending the next hours with his cattle. Mostly I didn't
get to go with him in those four- and five-year-old years, having to
content myself with playing cowboy for the hours of the day. But
most of life later, the pastures that run through the Mancos River
Valley still awaken me like almost nowhere else with their almost
magical geography.

People often ask me why I care about vocation as I do. I could
say a lot, I suppose, but more often than not I talk about my

grandfather. Watching him live his life first awakened me to the reality that life was more than labor, that vocation was more than occupation—but also that the work we do matters, matters very much. When I was ten, I didn't have those words or categories, but I began to think about things I never had before, especially about the meaning of the work we do.

In those summers of my boyhood I took the Santa Fe Chief, a train that once served Southwest America, from my home in California to New Mexico, an all-night trip across the great Mojave Desert through the vastness of northern Arizona, finally waking up in Gallup, the Navajo capital of America. My grandfather was there to meet me, and we would drive up the long road to Colorado, past Shiprock and more, coming to the livestock auction in Cortez before noon. And I remember him sitting in his truck before the sale began, listening to the stock reports—not the sale of commodities in Chicago or money in New York, but of cattle in Colorado.

One afternoon we were sitting beside each other in the sale barn, the colloquial name for a livestock auction, and the auctioneer, long a friend of my grandfather, was moving through his call, selling the livestock of the day. Sheep and goats, hogs and horses, then baby calves, their mamas, the yearlings and feeder cattle, and finally bulls. Along the way, he stopped, looking out onto the buyers of the sale barn, and asked my grandfather, "What are the price of these cows today?"

A question, an answer, only a few seconds. What was clear to me, even as a ten-year-old, was that the auctioneer knew that my grandfather would know the price, and he knew that my grandfather would be honest about it. My grandfather and I never talked about that interaction, but I listened and learned. Years later, I would use words like *competence* and *character* to describe my grandfather's reputation among his peers; though at the time I had nothing more than simple pride in my grandfather's life and labor.

In those years I spent my summer days with my grandfather and grandmother, taking into my heart the things they cared about. In a certain sense, what they cared about, I cared about, what mattered to them, mattered to me. And so when we watched *Gunsmoke* after supper, followed by family worship, it was written into my being that good people read the Bible, sang songs of love for God, and got on their knees to pray for everyone and everything. My grandparents were Scottish Presbyterians, coming from centuries of belief and behavior born of that tradition, and in their generation they lived into it with honest hope.

And I am their grandson, having taken their lives into my life. I didn't become a cowboy, though I still yearn for more of that world than is mine. But their place is still very dear to me, and given a good choice I would first choose the land where the mesas meet the mountains. When I decided to write the book that is now *Visions of Vocation*, I chose to place myself in their place while I wrote, beside a small creek not so far from where they lived, breathing their air, watching the aspens tremble just as they did.

A few years ago, Meg and I drove through Cortez and stopped by the sale barn. We looked around, seeing some sheep and an Angus bull, and not much more. (The sale day is Wednesday each week, and we were there on a Monday.) A man walked out, worn boots, Wranglers, a cowboy hat, wondering if he could help, and I told him that I had spent summer days there a long time ago. He asked me who my grandfather was, and I told him. With a big, wide, Western grin, he said, "Sure, I remember your grandfather" and went on to tell me stories that I knew and didn't know. We talked about years ago, about his own life working at the sale barn, about my grandfather and his friends. He named names of my grandfather's colleagues—cattle buyers from Denver to Albuquerque—that I hadn't thought of for most of my life. As we walked through the office, I saw a wall full of newspaper clippings, the stories of people I had known when I was ten—and I saw a whole row of lariats, coiled as working ropes would be, on the wall too. He must have seen my interest and asked, wonderfully he asked, "You want one?" Of course, I did.

Why do I think that vocation matters so much? While my grandfather spent years asking me questions, mostly about life and the world, wanting me to take both seriously, he never gave me a lecture on vocation. It is likely that he never used the word; I don't know. What he did was live a life, a coherent life, in which what he believed about God and the world was worked out in the way he lived in the world. Begun on his knees, he stepped into his work day by day over sixty years of cattle buying, contributing to his community with a far-ranging influence, offering an unusual blend of competence and character to the watching world. He was good at what he did, and he was also a good man.

In the years since that ten-year-old summer, I have come to call this "common grace for the common good"—and yes, I saw it first of all over my grandfather's shoulder and through his heart, learning the deepest lessons. The truest truths are always learned that way—even if we don't grow up to be cowboys.

Photo of me at a livestock auction in Cortez, Colorado.

OF WHAT WE DO AND WHY WE DO IT

AFTER A NIGHT AT THE MOVIES, I asked Meg, "Well, what did you think?" We talked for a while, back and forth, and eventually I said that the film was a surprising story of vocation, of what do we do and why do we do it.

For every one of us, that is complex—because we are complex. There is much to think about, much to account for, much to consider.

What I liked in *The Hundred-Foot Journey* is that the story reflects that complexity. Work matters, but it is not everything. Family matters, but it is not everything. Tradition matters, but it is not everything.

Set in the beautiful countryside of France, it is the story of an Indian family that left their homeland under duress, looking for a new place to call home. After finding England too wet, they settle in a quaint little French town that offers the possibility of beginning again.

The main character is the son who has an unusual gift of imagination and instinct, which he brings into being as a chef. As a boy his mother saw this in him and allowed him to see as she saw, to

40

smell as she smelled, to taste as she tasted. As a young man he takes his place in the family's restaurant, reclaiming the richness and pleasure of Indian cuisine for his French customers, but also taking the very best French food and making it better with tasty, spicy Indian accents, winning him attention from people near and far.

As his ability grows, as his fame broadens, he is invited to Paris, where he can compete at the highest levels—"haute cuisine," as they say. He flourishes in his labor but languishes in his life.

And it is here that the story is so very good. The young man wrestles with what he is doing, and why he is doing it; he wrestles with the meaning of his vocation. To see a story where the complexity of life is honored, and the importance of work is understood, is rare. The best stories are the truest stories, the ones in which we recognize ourselves, full of hope and honor, but also prone to self-deception and self-destruction.

Because *vocation* is a rich and complex word and is never the same word as *occupation*, we are always more than our work, though our work matters. This film celebrates work, but never romanticizes it. We create, but we sweat. We do our best but still disappoint. Sometimes, sometimes, heaven meets earth in and through our work, and it becomes almost sacramental—and then sometimes we curse the very work of work. We are our best and our worst at work.

My own first question about a film is always this: Did it tell a good story? I hate bad stories, cheap stories, ones that make us groan for all sorts of reasons. But when the credits rolled for *The Hundred-Foot Journey*, I watched them all the way through to the end, wanting to make sure I hadn't missed anything. Unlike so often, when the end of a film means a sigh of some sort, this time I was sure that I had seen a good movie—because it was a good story—because it told the truth about what we do and why we do it.

Image from *The Hundred-Foot Journey*, directed by Lasse Hallström (copyright: DreamWorks Studio, Glendale, CA, 2013).

COHERENCE AND
CONTINUITY MATTER

VOCATION **AND** *OCCUPATION*.

Two different but related words. There are few days when I am not drawn into a conversation with someone about the ways that these words orient us, forming who we are and what we do.

Not so long ago I had lunch with a long-time friend in Nashville who has been making music for most of his life, being a creative and prophetic voice for many people in many places. But things are changing for lots of reasons, and so we talked about what a vocation is and what an occupation is. The former is the longer, deeper story of someone's life, our longings and our choices and our passions that run through life like a deep river; the latter is what we do day by day, the relationships and responsibilities we occupy along the way of our lives, more like the currents in a river that give it visible form.

Every one of us has to make peace with the reality that in a now-but-not-yet world the two words and the realities they represent will never be exactly the same—even as we hope for more coherence between the two.

Coherence is part of the story, and continuity is as well. For every one of us, the things that we cared about when we were five-year-olds somehow make sense of what we cared about when we were sixteen-year-olds, just as the educational choices we made as twenty-year-olds connect with the vocational choices we make when we are thirty-year-olds. The dynamics that make us so unique and so different are like threads woven into the tapestry of a life.

For none of us, though, is it neat and clean. This was this, and that was that—therefore I spend my days as a butcher, a baker, or a candlestick maker. We make choices, and our choices have consequences; that is a true truth. But sometimes in a wounded world we make choices we don't really want to make, and sometimes there seems to be little relationship between what we long to do and what we end up doing. Even the creation groans.

Several years ago I was in Toronto as a guest on a television show focused on the challenge of the twenty-something years, especially of finding work we care about. Most of the time getting a job isn't so hard, but seeing our lives as a vocation is harder. That is as much a problem for Canadians as it is for Americans—and for Filipinos as it is for Italians and Kenyans. The challenge in the conversation in that evening was the challenge everyone everywhere faces, that is, connecting the deeper story of who we are with what we do, day by day, year after year.

A vocation is what my friend wants as he sees change coming; it is what we all want, in and through the transitions of life. It is why words like *coherence* and *continuity* matter. We yearn for the things we love to be the way that we live, even as we realize that the two will never be the same, completely and absolutely. We long for what we do to grow out of who we are, for our occupation(s) to be rooted in our vocation. That is the hope of everyone's heart.

Photo taken on a walk near our house along the tracks that go from Alexandria to Charlottesville. These same tracks once supplied the Union forces in Virginia and were blown up by the Confederate troops.

ORA ET LABORA

CAN WE HAVE A CONTEMPLATIVE LIFE and still live in Washington, DC? San Antonio? Austin? Dallas? Houston? San Angelo? Or how about Los Angeles or San Francisco, or Sacramento or Shafter? Do we have to leave life to find our lives?

From the desert fathers and mothers in the early centuries of anno Domini on through the escapes to Big Sur for the promise of high-priced Buddhism in our own day, we imagine it impossible to be people with an interior life who can account for the complexity and challenge of our exterior lives. The world seems too much for us. To live in it but not be of it seems beyond our ability.

Can we pray and work—*ora et labora*—at the same time?

St. Benedict began a long tradition of reflection on this almost fifteen hundred years ago. Discouraged by the cultural implosion of his own day—the decline and fall of the Roman Empire—he took up a life of disciplines that would keep his heart while he cared for the world. The hallmark of this Benedictine tradition was *ora et labora*, a life where praying and working were held together, offered as one heart and therefore one life.

They stumbled in their own way, from what I can read, and no one since then has figured it out with final clarity. We keep stumbling, longing for more coherent lives, where what we confess to believe looks like the way we actually live, where our deepest hearts are seamlessly worked out in the responsibilities and relationships of our lives.

Several years ago we were working at this in a retreat called "A Contemplative Life for the Rest of Life," at a place known far and wide as "a thin place," where heaven and earth meet in a remarkable way. In fact, to find one's way in requires the willingness to enter the waters of the Rio Frio, and I don't know what else to call it other than a sacramental experience, a baptizing of one's imagination, where the eyes of the heart are opened to see in a new way—at least if one has eyes to see.

As a young man, Howard E. Butt of the HEB Grocery Company in Texas wanted a place to work at this very question—Can I pray and work at the same time?—and because of hopes and resources that were his, he brought the Laity Lodge into being along the banks of the Rio Frio Canyon sixty years ago, and for generations now it has opened its doors with an unusual hospitality.

And now I have taken up this question, asked one more time, reflecting on the complexity of its challenge, offering the insights of Augustine of Hippo and John Bunyan, of Margaret Magdalene and Alexander Schmemann, of William Wilberforce and Abraham Kuyper, and of Leo Tolstoy too, each someone with a rare wisdom about the meaning of life in the world. The most important questions are perennial questions, asked and asked again, because they matter—whether we live in the fifth century or the twenty-first century, whether we are African or Russian, whether we are men or women, whether we are tinkerers or prime ministers. They are human questions because human beings ask them.

To see seamlessly is the hope, perhaps even to see sacramentally, where we have eyes to see where heaven and earth meet—where *ora et labora* become one—right in the middle of our ordinary lives, lived as they must be in ordinary places. At the end of the day none of us can live at Laity Lodge for the rest of life, as much as we might wish otherwise. If we are going to have contemplative lives that serve the world, they will have to be lived in the Washington, DCs, the Vancouvers, the Austins, and the Shafters, as well as the Jakartas, the Bratislavas, and the Nairobies of this world—at least that has to be true for most of us most of the time.

May it be so.

Photo of the Rio Frio at Laity Lodge, Texas.

SEEING SEAMLESSLY

"SO HE HAD LIVED IN CHILDHOOD and adolescence in the same country rectory, taking part each Sunday in a familiar liturgy which reflected, interpreted and sanctified the changing seasons of the farming year."

Reading one more novel of P. D. James—a master of murder mysteries who understands us, glorious ruins that we are, knowing the way things should be, even as her stories were about the way things should not be—I was struck by her simple description of seeing seamlessly.

Why and how do we learn to see heaven touching earth all around us, in and through every square inch of the whole of reality? For her, it was from a life where liturgy and labor were not finally different, but worship and work were intertwined, weaving a tapestry that gives us eyes to see the way things ought to be, even as we take into our hearts what is so painfully not supposed to be.

The best art always does that, and good books are one window into what that means, page after page drawing us into the truth of the human condition, facing as we must our dignity and our shame. Mysteries are always that story, and murder mysteries even more so. They are good stories only because they take us into the heart of our hearts, requiring that we ponder the perplexity of desire, the complex nuances of imagination and motivation.

This is never romanticism but rather honest wrestling with the fact of our humanness, wonderfully imagined and yet terribly hurt, every one of us. Made in the very image of God, and yet and yet, able and capable of the most horrific decisions with the most heart-wrenching consequences, we are disposed to dualisms that drive wedges between heaven and earth.

"A masterful writer" was the *Wall Street Journal*'s description of her gift. The *New York Times* described *Devices and Desires* as "better than her best." Through the years of her writing, she found ways to tell tales the whole world wanted to hear. And it is fascinating that she resisted compartmentalizing her life and work, her beliefs about the world from the way she lived in the world—in fact, to press the point, her deepest convictions about God and the human heart shine through the stories of frail human beings who live in this frail world, longing for lives that are impossible to find apart from grace.

When someone like James simply says that that her chief detective, Adam Dalgleish of Scotland Yard, learned to see sacramentally, she reminds us that the truest vocations are formed by a seamless understanding of life, torn as we are—as he was—by the painful reminders of our bent hearts, our mysterious capacity for twisted and wounding choices, even as we long for something more.

Whether our work is agricultural or academic, whether we are plumbers or carpenters, whether our labor is the law or the marketplace, whether our days take us into hospitals or schools, we want what we do with our lives to be born of something more, reflected, interpreted, and sanctified by the liturgical rhythms and realities of the truest truths of the universe. We are called to be like the Creator himself, yearning for heaven and earth to touch in and through the work of our hands.

Photo of a family at work gathering the summer hay in the Swiss Alps near the village of Gimmelwald.

VOCATIONS AS
SACRAMENTAL
SIGNPOSTS

LIKE ALL OF LIFE, and the history of every people and every place, the story of California is a complex one, even a messy one. On the one hand, what we know best is from the perspective of the Europeans who came from Spain in the seventeenth century. Some were missionaries like Father Junipero Serra, who walked from his ship in the gulf of what we now call Mexico to the capital city of New Spain, Mexico City, up through Baja California into Alta California, beginning in San Diego on the north, establishing missions in San Juan Capistrano, Santa Monica, Santa Barbara, and more, finally to San Francisco.

But it is also the story of Spain as a colonizing power whose reach extended into the "new world" with hopes for resources of all kinds to empower their king. That meant Serra's travels included the Spanish military, who brought their influence into the little outposts of the Church along the California coast, meeting earlier explorers and settlers who had found their own "new world" centuries earlier, immigrating from Asia over the Bering Straits down into North America. Whose home was it? From the very beginning it was messy, and there is no other history than that.

In truth, it is not altogether different than the Greece of Alexander the Great, whose empire extended throughout the known world of the time, overpowering whomever and whatever he found in the fourth century BC; or the Roman Empire of a century or so later whose power ruled the Mediterranean world with might for the next centuries, even extending itself through the European continent across the small sea to the British Isles; or of the Polynesian peoples who found their way to Hawaii fifteen hundred years ago, spending the next centuries fighting, killing, and cannibalizing, sacrificing children and women by the thousands to satisfy their "gods" of power and might; or the Vikings of twelve hundred years ago whose plundering, murdering, and raping of Scotland and Ireland over centuries make them sound to our modern ears like Scandinavian barbarians, the ISIS of their day.

In our very modern world, we romanticize some stories, missing the mess of history.

But Serra's story was different too, critically so, with a vocation born of a deeper justice, a deeper mercy, walking back to Mexico City to argue for the protection of the native peoples, trying to find a way forward for everyone who wanted a home there. He had eyes to see the sorrow that came with his coming, compounded by the sorrow that was already present in the centuries of aggression and violence of "the first nations" of California, and that too is the history.

Some time ago, I publicly reflected on these early years of what we now know as California, lingering for a while over its capital city, Sacramento, on my way to an argument for a sacramental vision of life and learning and labor, speaking first to a gathering of folks in the church and the marketplace, and then to a university faculty. Pointedly, I observed that in the generation after Serra, the Spanish captain Gabriel Moraga explored the hills on the eastern side of the great bay, what we now know as Oakland and Berkeley, wondering what might be beyond. With his soldiers, they found a great valley graced by the great mountains we now call the Sierra Nevada, full of flowers and trees, birds and fish, sunshine and blue sky, exclaiming, "Es como el sagrado sacramento!" *This is as beautiful as the holy sacrament!*

From that amazing moment, we have the city of Sacramento, capital of California—and so in my lectures in San Diego and Los Angeles, I chose to begin with the history that still shapes the people and their place. One cannot make sense of California in the twenty-first century without remembering to remember its missional history. The architecture itself tells the tale, with clay-tile roofs almost everywhere, adobe-colored buildings in cities small and large, and bells and more bells ringing through the generations across the Golden State, "Es como el sagrado sacramento!"

Not surprisingly, I spent my time working out a way of seeing seamlessly, which I argued was only possible if we see "sacramentally." Drawing on the biblical tradition, as well as the work of the contemporary French philosopher Simone Weil, I wanted my audience to understand that dualisms of every sort betray us because we imagine a chasm between heaven and earth that does not exist, seeing some things as "sacred" and some things not. We think that worship and work are fundamentally different—one being more important to God than the other, one being "spiritual" and one being "secular." Rather, if our truest vocation is the imitation of Christ, the very image of God, we see that everyone and everything matters, sacramental as it all is, holy as it must be. In a thousand ways our human experience of life in the world should be a window into the mystery and wonder of the reality of heaven touching the reality of earth, a "sacrament" so to speak, if we have eyes that see.

And that is always the issue for us, frail, fallen human beings that we are. Do we have eyes that see? Father Serra did, naming his missions after sainted folk, remembering them in hope for what might be. Captain Moraga did too, naming his moment with the grace of the holy sacrament, seeing even and especially the small things of life as holy. Ordinary people in ordinary places they were, but each had eyes to see more meaning written into the meaning of who they were and what they did.

That is our task too, ordinary people that we are, living in the ordinary places that are ours, called to see all of life sacramentally, understanding our vocations as signposts for a more coherent world where things that are real and true and right are woven into the fabric of the world—eating and drinking, worshiping and working, loving and living—seamlessly connecting the world that is with the world that someday will be.

With the mess that is mine—with the horrors of history that we bear, with the sorrows that sometimes overwhelm—I live my life for that.

Photo of the Mission Inn in Riverside, California.

WHEN A DREAM
BECOMES A LIFE

DREAMS ARE STRANGE THINGS. The stories that run through our souls at night are more often than not impossible to recollect; it's hard to remember them for ourselves, much less explain them to someone else. But there are other kinds of dreams, the ones that animate us for life, threading their way through who we are and how we live. They too can be difficult to discern, but they are the most trusted paths in life because they are the truest visions of vocation we have.

Over the course of fifty years, Thomas Edison, America's most prolific inventor, developed more than one thousand patents. When asked how it felt to have failed so many times in his decade-long efforts at the invention of the light bulb, Edison simply said he had not failed, he'd "just found 10,000 ways that will not work." His imagination and creativity drove him to persist—over and over, again and again.

I thought of all this watching the film *Joy*. The story by David O. Russell, whose earlier films include *Silver Linings Playbook* and *American Hustle*, is a remarkably insightful account of creativity and imagination, of gumption and grit, together forming a vocation in the life of Joy Mangano (played by Jennifer Lawrence). Yes, there is a quirkiness to the film, which Russell intends, but I found myself increasingly intrigued by the way Joy's earliest dreams of what she would do and how she would do what she did played out through the years of her life.

The movie begins with a conversation between Joy and her older sister. Showing a paper house she has imagined and built, Joy is explaining "This is this" and "That is that" to her older sibling who obviously is interested but also sad that she has never created anything like that, never imagined anything like that. Forty some years later, after 10,000 tries and facing crises and difficulties that are painful to watch, involving the complexities of a frail family and frustrating work, Joy finally finds her way into an idea that makes sense to the world around—and the camera allows us to see her looking into the little box with her paper world still intact. She remembers, and we do too. "I'm still that little girl, dreaming of the world I want to live in. I'm still that little girl, creating and imagining, describing to myself what I love and why I love it."

The wisest people I know see these early seeds in our souls as ones that matter for understanding the choices we make over the years of our lives. How else do we explain that in one family, born of the same parents and shaped by the same circumstances, such different people come forth? Why is one a scientist and one an artist, one an entrepreneur and one an athlete? Why does one love to dance, one love to sing, and one love to draw? Why does one, from her earliest days, see herself as a helper of people in need and one cannot not see the world around without imagining houses and streets and neighborhoods? Why is one a writer and one a chef? The differences only go on and on.

My best shot is that our hearts and minds, souls and strengths, are very different, uniquely so. Vocations are not occupations, though they are integrally woven together. To know the difference and the difference it makes is critical, and much of the grief we experience is born of mistaking one for the other. Vocation is always the longer, deeper story of someone's life. For Joy, she was always the creative creator of things she would make that the whole world would someday enjoy. Occupation is not that, but more the way we describe the things we do along the way of life, entering into particular responsibilities and relationships that are ours; while shaping and forming us, they are more often than not signposts of the deeper vocation. They are not the point; they point to the point.

One reviewer of *Joy* began with these words, "It's a Cinderella story, complete with mop." Yes, all the way through, that is this story, telling the tale of the girl who struggled and struggled, again and again, but who finally invented the Miracle Mop, selling her dream to the world. Not all of us find our way to fortune, even with hope and hard work. It is a broken world, and we are broken people. But we are all dreamers, longing for lives that are about something that matters.

This is what vocation is for everyone everywhere, a calling to care about the way the world is—even dreaming dreams about what might be—and working through the days of our lives at what could and even should be.

Image from *Joy*, directed by David O. Russell (copyright: Twentieth Century Fox, Los Angeles, 2015).

WAKING TO THE
MORNING LIGHT

THE GRAPES OF WRATH have come and gone from the San Joaquin Valley, but hopes and dreams, justice and mercy, loves and longings are still being worked out, day by day and year after year, in the long rows that make this the Golden Valley of the Golden State.

Good people still do good work on this good earth. With its sunshine, deep, rich soil, and water—sometimes water—anything and everything grows here. Melons, cotton, safflower, hay, almonds, carrots, oranges, and so much more. A contemporary cornucopia.

Most of us who walk into our Safeways, Krogers, Giant Eagles, Whole Foods, HEBs, and more all across America, never ever imagine that our food is grown by someone somewhere. We simply assume that the shelves will be full of our daily desires.

But each melon, each almond, each orange is brought into being by someone who loves the land. Spending the years of my boyhood here, imagining that the Central Valley was the center of California—two hours from anywhere I might imagine wanting to be, from the Sierras to the Pacific, from the Mojave Desert to Disneyland—I learned to love the smell of soil and even loved getting my hands dirty in its dirt. Contrary to the assumption of those who disdain the "backwards" character of the California that is neither Los Angeles nor San Francisco, I loved living in the land that fed the world. From my first years of adolescence on through my first years of adulthood, my summers were spent harvesting the crops that made California famous the world over. I loved the work, hot as it always was, backbreaking as it sometimes was.

But *love* is a strange word. More than romanticism, as that is not sustainable, love is a word that speaks of commitment and care, of affection and respect, and that can be as true of a person as of a place.

Years ago I remember driving along the country roads of the Valley with my father who had spent most of the years of his working life as a scientist for the University of California, studying the ways that plants grow well, and don't. A plant pathologist by training, he was a careful researcher, giving years to understanding verticillium wilt, a curse on the young seedlings that sprouted every spring throughout this fertile valley. The farmers depended on his work, listening to his analysis, trusting his instincts, investing their futures in his judgments. One evening he wanted me to see some of the places where he was working, where "plots" were given over to particular research questions. So we made our way along lonely roads, watching the last hours of the day's light filter across the fields. I still remember him saying that "it wasn't possible to pay someone to love the land"—at least that was his conviction, watching farming unfold over the years of his life and labor.

He wasn't wishing for a world that wasn't; that wasn't him. Instead, he was describing what he had seen of farmers and farming in the remarkably fruitful San Joaquin Valley, arguably the most productive farmland in the world. His work was among people who were small and large farmers, sometimes offering his service to large corporations too. Given that his employer was the university, he did not pick and choose those he wanted to serve; everyone had access to my father's insights.

But he noted that there was something different—and the difference made a difference—about those who loved the land they labored over. Of course, there was an economic reality for everyone: unless their crops made a profit, they would no longer be in business, whether they loved the land or not. But there was more to it than that. The willingness to work all hours of the day and night over the years of one's life was born of love, of deeply-wrought commitment and care, of undying affection and respect. And that work is the work of a farmer. There are no time clocks, there is no one to know whether you come to work in the morning or whether you work hard throughout the day. To love the land means that you work at your work whether anyone is watching or not—because as is true in the rest of life, love makes it possible to keep on keeping on.

Big business has tried to bring its techniques to California agriculture, and mostly it has been a failure. Where its footprints are visible, the land suffers. Too much is asked of it. Rather than stewardship for the sake of love and the future, the calculus is more a short-term profit maximization, and asks, "How much can we squeeze out of the land this year?" Because the land is so productive, this kind of farming "works" for a while, but it leaves a weary tale of worn-out people and a worn-out place.

But not everyone sees the world that way, and not everyone farms that way. Most are people of honest integrity, seeing their responsibility for the future of their families and communities—and so loving the land they farm. Overwhelmingly, these were the men and women of my life. Grandfathers and grandmothers, fathers and mothers, sons and daughters. Their world was my world.

And their ways remind me of the wisdom of Wendell Berry, who long has been a critic of the industrialization of agriculture wherever it is found. In a conversation on his front porch, he once said to me, "If you want to make money for a year, you have to ask certain questions. But if you want to make money for a hundred years, you have to ask other questions." That is as true in Kentucky as it is in California, and it is as true of businesses in the city as it is of farming in the country.

Do you love the land? There may be other questions that matter, but that one is critical, at the very core of good farming wherever it is done. My father's observation still rings true. Of all that I don't remember of my father's words, I remember his wisdom about the world of my growing up, that somewhere men and women have awakened to the morning light, taken up their vocations one more day—and in working to care for their land, bring food to our tables.

That is a gift.

Photo of the southern end of the San Joaquin Valley, looking toward the Tehachapi Mountains.

A DISPOSITION
TO DUALISM

WE ALL HAVE A DISPOSITION to dualism in our hearts.

One morning I was standing in a large circle of folk in Birming-ham's 16th Street Baptist Church gathered for what was called "a holy and historic moment" for the city, a prayer breakfast drawing black and white together for the sake of the city, hoping for the flourishing of their city. Hand in hand we sang "Amazing Grace"— "I once was blind but now I see"—with honest longing in our hearts, painfully aware of what the city has been, yearning for what the city can be and should be, gathered in a church building tragically known for the worst in the human heart, the malicious bombing that killed little girls in the midst of the civil rights tension of the 1960s. The former chief of police for Birmingham, an African American woman, led us in song, which itself seemed a remarkable window into what has changed in the city; no longer Bull Connor bullying his way through town, but the great-great granddaughter of slaves given the responsibility for the city's safety. A hint of hope in every important way.

But from beginning to end, I was struck by the irony of history too, the ironies of providence written into the song being sung in that place by those people. In the very room where we were meeting was a glass case with a model of a slave ship, asking us to remember to remember what once was, the reality that every black person there was a descendent of someone who had been stolen away from an African home, chained to hundreds of others in the hold of a ship that made its way across the "Middle Passage" as the trip was called from Africa to America. Those who made it across the Atlantic were sold as slaves in the Savannahs of these United States; those who didn't were thrown overboard along the way, chattel as they are, disposable property as they were.

And as most everyone knows, John Newton, composer of "Amazing Grace," was a slave-ship captain. In our fantasies we imagine that he did the unimaginable and horrible before his conversion, but that soon after he came to faith he understood the wrong written into his work, "I once was blind but now I see," and then urged his young friend William Wilberforce to stay in politics and work for the abolition of slavery.

That would be a happier story. But from what we know from history, Newton kept at his slave trading for years, continuing to captain ships full of slaves while on the top deck leading other officers in the study of Scripture—seemingly unable to connect his worship and his work, his beliefs with his behavior.

For a thousand complex reasons of the heart, like Newton, we are disposed to dualism. We choose incoherence rather than coherence, a fragmented worldview over a seamless way of life. For example, painfully so in the political seasons of life, we are first of all liberals or conservatives, Republicans or Democrats, our social and political ideologies shaping our identities; then we are good Baptists too, good Catholics too, good Methodists too, and on and on and on.

What particularly struck me about the irony of singing Newton's song while in the room with the slave ship was the sober reminder that the work of thinking Christianly is hard work. We do not come to it naturally. We are disposed to dualism, to carving up our consciences to allow us to believe one thing and behave as if another thing is true. "Did God really say . . . ? Of course not!" is the temptation coursing its way through the human heart.

It was a long pilgrimage for Newton, perhaps twenty-five years, maybe longer. While he stopped slave trading some five years after his initial repentance, it was not until thirty years later that he made his first public statement, acknowledging his sorrow. "It will always be a subject of humiliating reflection to me, that I was once an active instrument in a business at which my heart now shudders."

I don't despise him for that. How could I possibly, so very clay-footed as I am? So very frail a man that I am? To learn to see clearly is a long and always difficult work—disposed to dualism that we are. We are idolatrous people, twisting our hearts and world to make our choices for autonomy more comfortable in our conflicted consciences. We will do what we want to do when we want to do it, almost always.

That it took thirty years for Newton to begin to recognize this strange grace is worth pondering. Blind as we are, hoping for sight as we do, most of the time the work of grace is more "slowly, slowly" as the Africans describe their experience of life in this wounded world. Grace, always amazing, slowly, slowly makes its way in and through us, giving us eyes to see that a good life is one marked by the holy coherence between what we believe and how we live, personally and publicly—in our worship as well as our work—where our vision of vocation threads its way through all that we think and say and do.

The Hebrews called this *avodah*, a wonderfully rich word that at one and same time means "liturgy," "labor," and "life." A tapestry woven of everything in every way. That is the world we were meant to live in, and that is the world that someday will be. But now, in this very now-but-not-yet moment of history, we stumble along, longing for grace that connects our beliefs about the world with the way we live in the world. Over time, grace found Newton, transforming him heart and mind: "Now I see." May it be so for every one of us, blind as we are to our own disposition to dualism, hungry as we are for something more.

Photo of the stained-glass window in the 16th Street Baptist Church in Birmingham, Alabama; a gift of the children of Ireland to the church, remembering the bombing that killed the five girls.

A HARD QUESTION

A HINT OF HOPE—and sometimes that is all there is.

I gave a lecture in Charlottesville hosted by the Center for Christian Study, the "father" now of study centers throughout the United States. The center has a long history of offering resources of mind and heart for the students of the University of Virginia. My lecture asked, "Can We Know the World and Still Love the World?"—not a surprising question for anyone who knows me, but it is always a hard question, one that is asked from my heart.

The main room was full of folk, mostly undergraduates, some graduate students, and a few faculty. As I am wont, I made an effort to step into the world they inhabit, believing that they were just like me. And so I first said something about my assumption in coming into the room: we have all been hurt; we all have known sorrow; we all have experienced the wounds of the world. I don't wonder about that, but I simply assume it is true for everyone everywhere.

And in that we are not alone. So I told the story of Walker Percy, a son of the South whose family was torn asunder by the suicides of both his grandfather and his father. Before he was out of adolescence, his mother died too, of what was always seen to be mysterious circumstances; that is, her car was found in a levee outside of town, and no one ever knew whether she intended the "accident" or it "just happened." After his own undergraduate years at the University of North Carolina, he went to medical school at Columbia University. But before he began his residency, he contracted tuberculosis and eventually had to give up his plans to become a physician. Over the next twenty years he tried and tried to find a way forward—without much success. The world had been hard on him, losing both parents and his professional plans. What would he do now? Was there anything to do?

At age forty-five he wrote another story, hoping that someone somewhere would read it. And surprise of surprises, *The Moviegoer* won the National Book Award for Fiction, and that honor catapulted him into a place of prominence he never left. Over the next years he wrote several apocalyptically themed novels, *The Last Gentleman, The Second Coming, Love in the Ruins, The Thanatos Syndrome*, and more. Once asked about his willingness to look the bleakness of the human condition in the eye, Percy responded, "Yes, I will do that . . . but there is always going to be a hint of hope in my work too."

A hint of hope.

I spent some time that night on the heartaches of the world, pondering songs and songwriters who have artfully mourned for the sake of the world—from the Smashing Pumpkins to the Fray to Mumford and Sons. I even invited the students to choose a sorrow from that week. Would it be the martyrs in Libya, the burning to death of the Jordanian pilot, the murders in Paris? Or more locally, what about the Rolling Stone article on the rape culture at UVA, the story that wasn't true, and yet tragically and horribly is true. I wasn't trying to be mean but rather to have them think hard with me. Knowing what we know about the world, what will we do? How will we respond?

Can we know this world and still love it?

Most of the time we mused over the possibility of a way of knowing that implicates us, for love's sake, in the way the world turns out. A knowledge that means responsibility and a responsibility that becomes care. And of course I told several stories of former UVA students I have known and loved, who, having spent their years at Mr. Jefferson's university, are now working out their lives in the midst of the messiness of the world—its sociological and historical complexities, its economic and financial complexities, its medical and military complexities.

In their different ways, each is someone who understands life as a vocation, a life offered in service to the world born of a love for God. In their distinct ways, each is someone who sees their life as a way of answering the question of the night. Yes, in their own unique ways, each is a hint of hope—and sometimes that is the best we get.

Photo of the pavilions on the lawn at the University of Virginia.

ASSUMING COHERENCE

ONE MORNING I spent a couple of hours in a Google Hangout with several people in Chicago, taking part in a dissertation proposal meeting, hoping on hope that one day a PhD would be granted for the completion of good work well done. I was asked to participate because the student has drawn on ideas I have written about; the focus of her work for the degree has been the focus of my work.

At one point, her dissertation adviser commented that something she had written showed "conceptual congruity," an image that intrigued me. For most my life I have been drawn to the vision of coherence, believing in the deepest possible way that that is the truest truth of the universe. There is an intended seamlessness to human life under the sun. If we have eyes to see, there is congruity, and our task is to make sense of what is there. Life is meant to be coherent—but we don't experience it that way. All day long we live with incongruity and incoherence, with fragmentation across the whole of life. In families, among friends and neighbors, socially, politically, economically, between nations, and most tragically in our very souls.

We long for something more—with all of creation, we groan.

The very next morning I read an essay by Wendell Berry, "Discipline and Hope," in which he reflected on the possibility of "a continuous harmony." I've read most of what he's written a couple of times, but I think this is one of his best. The subtitle of the book is "Essays Cultural and Agricultural," a relationship worthy of our attention. Not surprisingly, he argues that we miss something crucial to our humanity—to our understanding of culture and of our cultural responsibility as human beings—when we lose contact with farms and forests, because it is there where it is more possible to see "a continuous harmony." Sun, soil, water. Spring, summer, fall, winter.

For the land to flourish, human beings must remember to remember their rootedness in the humus; in fact our responsibility is to steward the continuous harmony that is meant to be. When we forget, assuming that it doesn't really matter anyway, we flounder, and nothing works well for anyone or anything. Pastures and meadows, yes. Streams and rivers, yes. But economies too, local and global—and cities and societies as well. All of life, for everyone everywhere.

So, two mornings: conceptual congruity and continuous harmony. Years ago a mentor persuaded me that the best thinking—careful, critical thinking at its most skilled—assumes coherence. Rather than accepting fragmentation as normative, we should do the harder work of discovering and discerning the integral character of life and learning—and *integral* of course assumes coherence. The task becomes not so much "integrating" this with that, belief with behavior, ideas with life, but rather praying and thinking and working our way toward life as it's supposed to be, and in a profound way, is.

The issue then becomes having eyes that see, and seeing is never morally neutral. Always and everywhere it is morally directive, shaping our vision of what is real and true and right. And that's as true of the most ordinary things in your life and mine, as it is of PhD dissertations.

Photo of an aspen leaf just as fall is falling in Pagosa Springs, Colorado.

WHAT MAKES
A GOOD LIFE?

SOMETIMES WORDS write themselves on our hearts.

I still remember a conversation with a friend we had invited to join us for lunch, and we were talking about anything and everything. He was one of the bright lights of life: smart, personable, gifted.

"Sometimes I feel like sixteen different people." A serious actor full of hope that he would spend his life on stage taking up roles and characters to satisfy his yearnings and pay his bills—but for many reasons, all tragic, that never happened. In those years I was studying psychology, especially the ways that philosophical anthropology affects psychotherapy, and so I was intrigued by what he said. What we believe about who we are and why we are is the root of everything else, and we will either find honest happiness in this now-but-not-yet world or we will fall down and fall apart.

All of us long for integrity, for an identity that makes sense of ourselves to ourselves—but for thousands of complex reasons we stumble along, often feeling more fragmented than coherent; often in fact making choices that take us step by step to incoherence. In the end we don't really know who we are and why we are.

All this came to mind when we saw *Birdman*, the film by the gifted director Alejandro González Iñárritu. The story is of a film star trying to finally make it on Broadway, an actor who has made millions as "Birdman," a fantastical character in a film world of fantastical characters—Batman, Superman, Incredible Hulk, X-Men, Fantastic Four, and on and on—but who longs for a kind of acting that only happens on the stages of Broadway.

Michael Keaton is the Birdman, an aging actor who feels he has one last shot at being someone who has done something. His fame and fortune were made as a bird-man—with feathers and talons and beak—and while that had been "him" for the years of his stardom, it had never really been him. How could it have been?

And so he comes to New York City, the city of stages and stories, bright lights and great hopes. There is much that could be said about the film, and many have written about it. What interested me was the way that identity was lost and found and lost again—which of course reminded me of the tender and complex conversation with our friend so many years ago. There were moments when the dialogue was almost eerie, an echo of what we heard from our friend.

Who are we? How do we know? What makes for a life? For a good life? What matters when all is said and done?

In an interview, director Alejandro González Iñárritu said this about his main character and the existential quandary that is the heart of the film:

> That's the story of every human being. I always thought of this guy as Don Quixote in that sense. We're all like that. We have these ambitions that are very hard to accomplish because life puts us in our place. We have this battle with mediocrity. Everyone's terrified of being mediocre. Everyone wants to be special. We parents tell our kids, "You're special." But how many people *are* special? Very few people are special. Everybody wants to be special. And they have been selling us that poison. That's tragic and comic.

On the one hand, I have always believed in Fred Rogers and his promise that "We are special"—everyone of us in our own unique way. But on the other hand, it is painfully and plainly true that we are all very ordinary people living very ordinary lives in very ordinary ways.

And yet and yet, written into every one of us is the longing to be special in some way, for some meaning in some way about some thing, for a significance that sets us apart from everyone else. We want our lives to be about something that matters, to have done something that matters to someone somewhere. That is the tension of life for Everyman and Everywoman—and that was our friend's hope, even torn apart as he was over the deepest questions of who he was and what he was, of why he was and how he was to live.

At the end of *Birdman*, I found myself thinking about many things, perplexed by what I had seen and what it meant. Not surprisingly, perhaps, the film *It's a Wonderful Life* began running through my mind with its story of George Bailey's own pilgrimage over the meaning of life. He too was faced with the great questions of who and what and why and how; we all know his story.

The heartache of *Birdman* is that it is formed by a profoundly different narrative; the questions are the same, but the answers are antithetical. (Even the best reviews, like in the *Atlantic*, give the story a pass here, not expecting it to make sense, and so of course Keaton's character doesn't have to make sense either.) Unlike George Bailey's world, there is no window to transcendence, and so no one is looking in and down from heaven on his life, and therefore there is no possibility of a holy visitation that will change the course of his life, the very way he understands human existence. The universe is silent.

At the end of his film, George is surrounded by a community of family and friends who gather round, singing a glad song that remembers to remember the truest truths of a good life. When all is said and done, all the Birdman has is himself, and at the end of the day and the end of the film, that isn't enough.

Heart-achingly, it wasn't enough for our friend either, perplexed and confused about the most important questions of his life as he was—just as it wasn't for the Birdman, troubled soul that he was. We all long for something more.

CARITAS AND THE
COMMON GOOD

WHAT IS THE COMMON GOOD?

We could, with meaning and richness and depth, ask, what is *caritas*? But to answer that question we have to come back into the very reason for the being of a university like the University of California, Berkeley, and of its origins in the seventeenth-century Anglican bishop George Berkeley's musings over the nature of knowledge. The best questions, the truest questions, are complex, and their answers are complex. Wondering about the common good takes us to "how do we know?" which presses into the deepest things of life—yours, mine, and everyone everywhere. These are the questions that human beings have always asked and always answered—and some answers are better than others.

A lecture I gave in Berkeley, California, explored who we are and what it means to live together in a pluralizing world. Sponsored by good people who are committed to the welfare of their city, this was the first effort they have made to work together, sponsoring a forum for speaking into the nature of the good life, for everyone.

Words like *good* are pregnant words, of course, full of all sorts of hopes and dreams, different and diverse as they might be. What is "good"? And what is "the common good"? In a pluralizing society, can we even speak about a common good? Or is our future only more fragmentation, more isolation, more tribalism?

Choosing to begin with memories deep within me of days spent on the Cal campus as a twelve-year-old, joining my father in his days there working with other UC scientists, him giving me a loose rein, allowing me the freedom to roam the university and city. And then my days as a college dropout eight years later, taking up what I even then called my "extra-academic education"—asking questions that college wasn't very able to answer—living in communes in both the Bay Area and Europe, learning hard but good lessons about "the common good."

Along the way I remembered Bishop Berkeley (whose name was the inspiration for the city and university), who was both an Anglican bishop and an Enlightenment philosopher, wrestling in his own time with the questions that still run through everyone's mind and heart; and the five UC professors who wrote *Habits of the Heart* a generation ago, studying the work of Alexis de Tocqueville a century and a half earlier about the whys and whats and wherefores of the American experiment, wondering what "habits of heart" would be required to achieve our promise as a people, a common good that was honest and sustainable over time; and Bernard of Clairvaux and Augustine too, drawing on their deep insights about what matters most for human flourishing for us as human beings to be what we can be and should be in our life together.

And before it was over, my friend Hans Hess and his hamburgers came into the story, as did my work with the Mars corporation in its efforts to develop a serious rethinking of the way business is done in the world, "the economics of mutuality" we have called it. And finally to my work with the Murdock Trust, a common grace for the common good foundation, serving all kinds of people in all kinds of ways throughout the Pacific Northwest. All windows into good people doing good work, vocations in service of the common good.

Caritas is a good word. From it we get charity and compassion, love and affection. The core of any meaningful conversation about the common good lies in that most important of all questions: What do you love? Our answer not only affects our selves but our societies. In the end, we are always choosing which loves mean the most and which don't, which loves matter and which don't.

Glorious ruins that we are, we are capable of great good and great evil, of glories and of shames, so that ordering our loves rightly is what makes the common, good—which matters for all of us.

Photo of the Sather Gate on the campus of the University of California, Berkeley. Built in 1910, this was the original entrance to the campus on the south from Telegraph Avenue.

DE PROFUNDIS

I WAS INVITED to give a lecture at Montreat College in North Carolina. The college received funding from the Lilly Endowment to address the relationship of education to vocation, a project the foundation has generously supported for many years; Lilly has given over $200 million to this and obviously thinks it matters for who we are and how we live.

The planners chose four speakers to address four themes, each one grounded in the Story that makes sense of all stories, the meta-narrative of creation-fall-redemption-consummation. Every human being on the face of the earth asks and answers questions that arise from this view of history—whether we buy into its commitments about life and the world or not, wondering, *Where did all this come from? What happened? Can it ever change? What is the end of history?* These are the questions of every life, for everyone everywhere.

I was asked to take up the second question: What happened? Why are things such a mess? Why is there horror and injustice and suffering? Why do we weep? Why do we groan? In their different ways, they are one question, of course.

As I pondered this question for myself, one of the poetic windows I looked through was from the band Mumford and Sons, and their song "Hopeless Wanderer." As they put it, with simple, stark honesty, "But do not tell me all is fine."

Instinctively we know that. Intuitively we know that—and in thousands of ways we respond to its reality. Two very common answers are "karma is" and "shit happens," realizing as we do that we have to account somehow and some way for things not being as we want, as we expect, as we believe it should be.

But it is the "should be" part that makes it complicated. When we introduce *should* or *ought* into the conversation, even into our heart of hearts, we let our slips show, as not every story of life and the world can make sense of words like that. We need a meta-narrative that is rich enough and true enough, accounting for the complexity that we all know and feel in our very bones.

All of us, sons of Adam and daughters of Eve, have been thinking about this for a long time, from the beginning of time, in fact. The Buddhists decided to call it "emptiness," and embrace that as the point of life because it is life. Marx saw alienation everywhere, yearning for something more.

And in the last century, we have Albert Camus and his plague, Walker Percy and his getting lost in the cosmos, Shūsaku Endō and his silence, Bob Dylan and his world where everything is broken, Billy Corgan and his zero, and Johnny Cash and his hurt—in their own ways each one trying to make sense of what we all are trying to make sense of: *What happened?*

The composer Arvo Pärt and his "De Profundis" give voice to the ache of human beings through the ages: "De profundis clamavi ad te, Domine," *From the depths I cry to you, O Lord!* Though we do feel lost, we hope that all is not lost. From Psalm 130 on, with memorable stops along the way in the musical imagination of Martin Luther, on through the Polish death metal band Vader, we see the world and its wounds and cry out from the depths of our being. There is good reason to do that, knowing what we know of ourselves and others, of our lives and the world. But along with Mumford and Sons, we will not allow the romanticism that insists that this is the way it's supposed to be. We cannot repress reality that much—we can't if we are honest, because it hurts too much.

Photo taken at Assateague National Seashore, home of the wild ponies, on the Virginia coast.

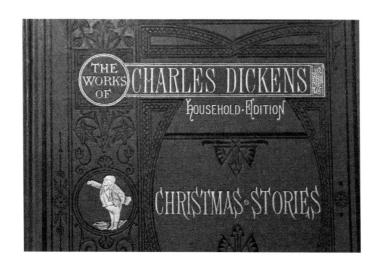

LAUGHING WITH THE DEVIL, LAUGHING WITH GOD

"**THE DEVIL LAUGHS** because God's world seems senseless to him; the angels laugh with joy because everything in God's world has its meaning."

When I first read those words, I was struck by their hard-won wisdom. Milan Kundera, one of the great novelists of the twentieth century, wrote about the challenge of being human in the modern world, embodied in Prague under the weight of totalitarianism, the totalistic worlds and worldviews of Nazism and Marxism. Perhaps best known for *The Unbearable Lightness of Being*, his subject was always the world that Nietzsche had warned about a century and a half earlier— that when we lose God, we lose access to meaning and morality.

I have been deeply influenced by his writing, seeing his critique as profoundly and perceptively true of our time in history, so it was a surprise to read a short story by Charles Dickens, *The Battle of Life*, written in the mid-nineteenth century, and be reminded of Kundera. Many of us are profoundly formed by *A Christmas Carol*, but Scrooge and Tiny Tim only come once in this life. Dickens, master storyteller that he was, wrote time and again about the meaning of the season, each Christmas story full of people we know, perennial people, wrestling with the world, the flesh, and the devil like we are.

When I began reading I was struck by the beauty of his prose—as beautiful as I have ever read. In a strange juxtaposition, the first paragraphs are about a place of great horror and sorrow, a battlefield of the world, where countless men and horses lost their lives. With remarkable genius, Dickens requires that we remember the grief, even as we see the same ground with new eyes, when after generations the people no longer know the meaning of their place. Where men and horses are long buried, their flesh and bones one with the earth, stone cottages and rose-covered trellises now stand—and those who live in them have no memory of what once was. The change does not happen overnight, but slowly we no longer remember to remember.

At its heart *The Battle of Life* is about grace—which is why it qualifies to be included in "the Christmas stories." But Christmas and grace? How are they connected?

Because I care deeply about the relationship of ideas to life, of what we believe and how we live, the word *grace* is one that matters because its meaning is written into the very meaning of life. Like everything else in the world, we can misread it, which is why "cheap grace" should be protested, much as every one of us longs for it sometimes and some days. But there are other ways to distort the meaning of grace too, that is, by confusing it with other ways of life, other ways of seeing the world where grace does not and cannot exist.

Theists of every stripe often miss here, imagining instead that goodness makes a good life. The materialist West misses just as badly as the pantheist East; in their own distinct ways they argue instead for *karma*, that things are already "written," that the world is "hardwired," that we are "stuck in moments we cannot get out of," with thousands upon thousands of variations on that theme. Determinism is as against grace as is pantheism—which is of course why the poet of Dublin sings, "Grace is beyond karma, beyond karma." Ideas have legs, always and everywhere, and so karma has meaning, just as grace has meaning, but what they mean are universes apart.

Christmas, if it is about anything, is about grace. Scrooge was not stuck forever. In the great mystery of that long night, heaven came to earth, offering him another way of seeing himself and his world. Dickens did not offer a fully developed theology of salvation, reflecting for his readers on the meaning of the birth and life and death and resurrection of Jesus; in fact, from what I have read of his thinking, he was not fully persuaded of all that we call "mere Christianity." But Dickens did see some things very clearly, offering rare insight into the reality of life in the world.

The Battle of Life is one more window into that gift. The story is of a widowed father with two daughters living in a stone cottage with a rose-covered trellis, built on the very earth of an awful, grievous moment of history. A physician by training, he is certain that life has no meaning and laughs with the devil "because God's world seems senseless to him." He responds to all things great and small with, "Ha-ha . . . because it's all silly," refusing to see anything or anyone as morally meaningful. There are reasons, because there are always reasons. But as the story unfolds through the years, his skepticism is challenged by a surprising grace, incarnate in the simple insight of a mostly illiterate maid who works in his home, a woman who can only read the words "Forgive and forget." Yes, a surprising grace, a strange grace. When the eyes of his heart are finally open, he says, "It is a world we need to be careful how we libel, Heaven forgive us, for it is a world of sacred mysteries, and its Creator only knows what lies beneath the surface of His lightest image."

There is a remarkable resonance between those last words of Dickens and "the unbearable lightness of being" of Kundera. But that should not surprise us, if we understand what the days of December mean. Christmas sets before human hearts the world over a line in the sand, a battle over the meaning of life. What kind of world is it anyway? And how will we live in it?

Karma is always an argument against moral meaning because, if it is true, we are not responsible, able to respond; grace argues differently. Against all odds, against every imagination and pretension, when we believe in Christmas we are believing that God is not silent, that in time and space grace has become flesh, inviting us to forgive and forget the heartaches of our own lives because we now see that a morally meaningful life is possible because "everything in God's world has its meaning," hard-won wisdom that it is.

When we choose against grace, we choose an "eye for an eye," committing ourselves to the survival of the fittest. The jungle works that way, but that is a world and worldview away from how most of us want to live, most of us need to live. Scarred by the battles of life, wounded by the world, we are like the characters of Kundera and Dickens laughing with the devil or with God—either believing that nothing matters or that everything matters in this world of "sacred mysteries." Like all things that matter most, it is a question of having eyes that see what is real and right and true, and what is not.

Photo of *Christmas Stories* by Charles Dickens, published in 1873.

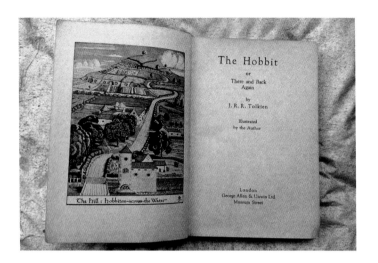

ON DUTY AND DESIRE

DUTY AND DESIRE.

A few years ago I spent some time at the Wade Center on the campus of Wheaton College—I only wish that I had had hours to ponder, taking its riches into my deepest places. There is no place like it on the face of the earth.

With the feel of an English cottage, it is the library for the collected works of George MacDonald, G. K. Chesterton, Dorothy Sayers, C. S. Lewis, J. R. R. Tolkien, and a few others. Not really a museum, it is a place for remembering the lives and literature of a remarkable group of people. Yes, there is "the wardrobe" with its door open to everyone's imagination, and there is the writing desk of Tolkien, but mostly it is a research library with stacks of books in beautiful cases, holding everything written by and about these authors.

I asked if they had a first edition of Tolkien's *The Hobbit*. With a smile and a nod, they told me that they had one in a special locked collection. "Would I like to see it?" Of course, I did. And a few minutes later the librarian returned with the book, a first edition with Tolkien's signature gracing its inside cover. What I wanted to do then was call off my day and simply sink into a chair and read.

But instead I made peace with a longing look and opened the first pages with Tolkien's drawings and his immortal first words, "In a hole in the ground there lived a hobbit." In ways that would probably surprise, I have taken the hobbits into my heart, allowing them to form and shape my own pilgrimage. Truth be told, I. Am. A. Hobbit.

The night before my visit to the Wade Center, I had given an address focused on vocation as integral to learning and life. Before it was over, I drew on Tolkien's moral imagination, his way with words that both delight and instruct. For a thousand reasons it seemed right—not only am I a glad apprentice to him in mind and heart but the school has honored him in its Wade Center, offering generations to come the opportunity to learn from his work.

I talked about duty and desire. While courses could be taught about the ways that hobbits and humans wrestle with the dynamic interaction between what we know is real and true and right, and the loves that form our desires to do what is real and true and right—to know and to do at the same time—I simply drew on a letter from Tolkien to his publisher to underscore the importance of seeing them together as the heart of a good life.

After the smashing success of *The Hobbit* on both sides of the Atlantic, Tolkien's publisher, Allen and Unwin, wrote to the professor, asking if he had "anything more about hobbits in mind?" You can imagine the weight of the question for those who had seen the book become a best seller and who hoped that there might be more!

He wrote back, reflecting on the tension of his own life with his family responsibilities and his teaching—the complexity of his own vocation—and said, "I begin to wonder whether duty and desire may not (perhaps) in future go more closely together."

For years I have mused over those words, certain that they account for the deepest things of the human heart.

We long for coherence, but we live with dissonance. We know what we should do, but we don't want to do what we should do. We know what is right, but we don't want to do what is right. The business of "want" and "desire" is at the bottom of everyone's being. As Václav Havel taught us, "The secret of our humanity is the secret of our responsibility." We are able to respond responsibly, and that is the core of our humanness. We are always responding to the world around us—knowing what we want and desire, we choose.

For a thousand complex reasons in your heart and mine, we find ways to recast the relationship between duty and desire, stumbling over ourselves and the reality of the universe—and there are consequences, for us as individuals and for our world. We become a bit less human, and life becomes a bit less than it should be and could be. And sometimes, sometimes, our choices have more weight because they are more tragic, full of heartache with far-reaching consequences for everyone everywhere.

There are implications for places like Wheaton too, of course, teaching as it does a way of life, a way of learning. At the end of the day, and at the end of an education, it is only when students long for the way of life and learning that is formed by what is real and true and right that they will flourish. That is the world that is ours, and we have no other world to live in.

Duty and desire—for Tolkien, for his hobbits, for all of us.

Photo of *The Hobbit*, first edition, at the Wade Center at Wheaton College.

UNBROKEN AND BROKEN

VIR.

It is not a word we use very often. But we do know *virile*, *virility*, and *virtue*—each is rooted in the ancient word *vir*. What is a man? What does it mean to be human? Who are we? What are we like? What are we supposed to be like?

Like thousands of others, I went to see the film *Unbroken*. Having read the book, I was intrigued when Angelina Jolie announced she was bringing the story into the cinema—and of course, I wondered what she would do with Louis Zamperini's life, the unbroken man who became so very broken.

The movie poster promises a story about survival, resilience, and redemption, and that is the amazing story that Laura Hillenbrand wrote in her incredibly researched, well-written biography. I was captivated—even if I was also horrified.

I still remember one Saturday morning reading in bed and leafing through pages. My good wife, Meg, who knows me well, said, "What are you doing? You don't read like that." She knows that I am a first-page-to-the-last-page reader, taking in everything from beginning to end—and so she wondered. I told her that I was just trying to see how much longer Zamperini and his buddies were going to be stuck at sea in a raft. After even a few days of following their travail, I was worn out, having no idea that they would be men at sea for forty-seven days!

I groaned when I saw that I had pages and pages left to read before they found land. But refusing to read ahead, I had no idea that being lost at sea was its own strange grace, as sighting land meant that they would now be prisoners of war, destined for long days and months suffering under the brutal oversight of the Japanese army.

Watching the film, I thought a lot about the virtue of resilience. It isn't cheap, and we cannot dismiss it as small. It is so very hard to keep at anything that matters; most of us don't. As Zamperini says again and again and again, "If I can take it, I can make it." The film only begins to account for the malicious treatment that he and his fellow prisoners experienced, but it tries. It was awful and tragic and horrible—and if we can take it, we will make it to the end of the film.

So what do we do with this story? The film is full of the glories and the ruins of the human condition, painfully presented. As one friend said to me, "It's not a very happy night out." But what does it mean for us?

For me, it raises several questions, all surrounding the strangely rich word, *vir*.

What does it mean to be a human being? A profoundly perennial question, we have been pondering this for a long time. Thousands of years ago, from the earliest sources we have, we read of people trying to answer this question. If *vir* means "man," then "virtue" points us in the direction of what it means to be a man, to our true end as human beings.

Vices take us in the other direction. Not "little vices" after all, the word *vicious* stands in relation to *virtuous*, just as *vice* does to *virtue*. When we see it that way, we realize that *vicious* is a harder word, always meaning something awful, something destructive, something that will hurt. It is important to understand that every virtue has a corresponding vice, and we either become more human, or less human, over the course of life. Flawed virtues keep us from flourishing, from being fully and wholly human, perverting us and having destructive consequences for everyone else.

Zamperini is offered as a man of rare resilience, of great courage. His chief tormentor, the "Bird," as he was known in the prison camp, was a man born by his bravado, his false courage, his twisted and distorted courage. Simply said, he was a vicious man, wreaking havoc and horror wherever he went, whatever he did.

When Jolie's story is done, we have spent a long time in the presence of a virtuous man, a remarkably "unbroken" man, as she offers him. Where her telling of the tale suffers is that she only nods at the brokenness, which is also integral to the story. With a few words of postscript, we hear something of what happened after the war, with Zamperini's descent into depression, his life imploding, his manliness breaking. At that critical point, Hillenbrand is a more honest storyteller, insisting that we pay attention to the longer, deeper, truer story.

In reality, none of us can "take it till we make it" in the push and shove of the wounded world that is ours. We fall down. We stumble. We are clayfooted. We not only see through a glass darkly but worse, we live through one too.

What does it mean to be human? The virtues point us in the direction of our true humanity, so justice, temperance, prudence, and courage show us the way to being human. But being courageous isn't enough at the end of the day; resilience, by itself, is stoicism, and that falls short of what it means to be fully human. As hard as it is to "take it"—and sometimes it is incredibly hard to take it, as this film shows—in the face of the ravages of the world, the flesh, and the devil, we need more, which is why the wisest ones have argued that faith, hope, and love are virtues that complete the story. They did so for Louis Zamperini, the unbroken man who became broken—broken as he was, his great need was to be made whole, holy and whole, and in that to become the human being he was always meant to be.

Survival. Resilience. Redemption. The movie poster got that right, and we should too.

Image from *Unbroken*, directed by Angelina Jolie (copyright: Universal Pictures, Universal City, CA, 2014).

A LONGING FOR GRACE

FOR A THOUSAND REASONS NEAR TO MY HEART, I find myself awakening to the poetry of U2's "Grace." Perhaps because it reminds me of the truest truth about me: that, in the words of Psalm 103, I am dust.

For years now the song has been a line in the sand for me. What Bono and his band are arguing, poets as they are, is that the universe is one way and not another, that life is one way and not another—that grace is not only "the name for a girl," but "a thought that changed the world."

Pressing the poetic point, the heart of the song is the contrast of karma with grace, setting forth the cosmic good news that we are not stuck. That things are not just the way they are. That things will not always be as they always will be. That the universe is not fundamentally indifferent to my deepest longings. Instead, grace travels outside of karma—and therefore as a human being I can make choices, and those choices, transformed by grace, make "beauty out of ugly things." Even and especially me, dust that I am.

I have been an eager and long student of Václav Havel, seeing in him a man of unusual vision and courage. Several years ago I flew into Prague, simply for the reason of wanting to walk on the streets that were his, to look up at the balconies from which he spoke, and if possible to talk with the citizens of the city about the man himself.

For reasons that grew out of his Czech history and the politics of his life, Havel spent years living into the conviction that "the secret of man is the secret of his responsibility." Paralyzed by history, the Czech people saw no way forward. And so in speech after speech, Havel gave himself to the political meaning of responsibility, of the ability to respond to the world around us. Simply said, but profoundly and politically meaningful, we are not stuck.

When the album "All That We Cannot Leave Behind" came out, and U2 toured around the world, I was invited to speak one evening before one of the concerts. A number of journalists were there, people who write for the wide world, each one intrigued by the celebrity and seriousness of the band. My task was to reflect on why U2's music mattered for all of us.

Among the songs, I lingered over "Grace," thinking aloud about the idea, about what it means, and what it does not mean. *Grace makes beauty out of ugly things.*

One of the journalists was puzzled. Thoughtful, articulate convictions about the whole of life, he said that he knew of nothing in his Jewish religious vision that could account for an idea like grace. "Nothing that I believe can make sense of that." As we walked to the concert, we kept talking about U2, and that song in particular. I remember thinking that I had never been in a situation so much like that of the apostle Paul in the first century, where the gospel of grace is "a stumbling block to the Jew." Grace cannot be.

As I watch the world, most of the time for most people, we do feel stuck in moments and lives that we cannot get out of. Intuitive artist that he is, Bono feels that in the world all around him, feeling the futility that karma is it, that things are as they are and always will be—unless there is grace. That transformation is not possible— "karma, karma" is the final truth—unless there is grace.

So I long for grace. I long for the possibility that what seems to be true is not true. That honest transformation of me and mine, of my life and the world, can happen, making beauty out of ugly things. I long for that.

Photo of Bono of U2 in concert in Pittsburgh, Pennsylvania.

BEING IMPLICATED

A LONG TIME AGO I spent a summer in the Valley of the Sun. Just graduated from college, I had chosen to study with a philosophy professor in Phoenix, a man whose Indian roots gave him unusual insight into the world and worldview of Southeast Asia. Believing that ideas had legs, his earnest, articulate passion about the ways that learning and life were twined together intrigued me.

So we spent the days of that summer reading, and in deep conversation about what we were reading. One of his gifts to me was that he understood the integral relationship of metaphysics, epistemology, and ethics; that is, what we believe about the world—What is real?—informs what we see in the world—What is true?—and that informs how we live in the world—What is right?

I still believe that, mostly at least.

And so a few years ago when I gave an address in Tempe to a group of good people from across America, literally from San Francisco to Boston, I began with the story of my summer in Phoenix, thinking through these questions and what they have meant for my life.

I was asked to speak from my book *Visions of Vocation* and was given this title, "On Being Implicated." As I thought through what I should say, I remembered again the ways that these three questions are ours, all of us. Self-conscious or not, we live our lives in their light. We cannot not.

Most of life later, I think the questions and the ways we answer them play back-and-forth upon each other with complexity and mystery. We are not, first of all, philosophers, consciously theorizing about the universe—even philosophers are not that. Human beings that we are, we are choosers, choosing how we will live. It is our longings and loves that form us, most deeply forming what we believe about what is real and true and right with *complexity* and *mystery*. And so there are no cheap answers to the questions of life because there are no cheap questions about life, and if we imagine otherwise, we are badly mistaken.

On being implicated? Of course I set before them the intensity of the challenge of living in a messy world. Broken and bent, wounded and hurt, we are and our world is. How do we make sense of ourselves in it? None of us can be content with contemporary accounts that allow us to say, "Of course I know that, but who cares?"

I offered the Hebrew vision of knowing instead, a knowing that implicates us, for love's sake, in the way the world turns out, in the way that we turn out—listening to Abraham Heschel and the prophetic tradition, musing over the word *yada*. But then we stopped along the way with Simone Weil and the very last words found in her notebook the morning after her death: "The most important task of teaching is to teach what it means to know." And finally remembering the story we call "the good Samaritan," asking what it means to learn to pay attention, to see ourselves implicated in what is real and true and right.

To give flesh to my words, I told a bit about my friends Hans Hess and Todd Deatherage and the different ways they have seen themselves implicated, responsible for love's sake, for the way the world is and ought to be. Yes, it is worth trying to make burgers the way they're meant to be—for example, Hans's Elevation Burger—and, yes, it matters to work for the peace of Jerusalem—for example, Todd and Telos.

When we see our lives in this way, we begin to understand the vision of vocation, what is ours to love in this life, what is ours to care about, living as we are stretched taut between the way things ought to be and the way things someday will be.

That I am still working away at questions that were mine so many years ago sometimes seems strange to me, that is until I remember to remember that this has become my vocation. This has been mine to care about in and through the work that has been mine. The questions mattered to me as a young man, trying to understand the world and to find my place in it—and they still do, surprisingly perhaps. I have spent my life living into those questions, seeing that they were not just mine, but were ones asked by every son of Adam and daughter of Eve, by everyone everywhere.

Photo of a cactus on Camelback Mountain in Phoenix, Arizona.

FRIENDSHIP ISN'T
SECOND BEST

MOST OF LIFE AGO I was an adolescent, making my way through years of awkwardness, the years when we begin to be aware of ourselves as selves, full of wonder about everything. No longer a boy, not yet a man, I was beginning to be interested in the girls of my life—and what seemed clear, the more I thought about it, was that were two kinds of girls, "friend" girls and "girlfriend" girls.

As I became more serious about what I believed about life and the world and why I believed it to be true to the way the world really is, the first thing I rethought was girls. Who were they? Who was I in relation to them? What should an honest and true relationship be like if it wasn't marriage? With sorrow in my heart, I realized that I had stumbled badly, missing the meaning of the girls I had known.

Over the next years of my life I gave a lot of thought to that, sure that if I couldn't make sense of what I thought most about in light of what I believed, then nothing else would make sense either. If I couldn't understand girls, then how was I going to understand politics, economics, the arts, education, and everything else?

That still seems true.

The first person to embody that question was Meg—in a surprising and unusual way the challenge to my autonomy became incarnate in her and in the friendship we began to have over the next several years. I wanted to see her differently. I wanted to understand her more completely in light of what I was coming to believe about God, about the world, about life and love.

One of the commitments I began to work out was that friendship wasn't second best. I could no longer say of some girls, "Oh, don't be stupid! She's just a friend!" And thereby dismissing them as ones that I didn't really care about, as girls who were "just friends."

I never got this all done well. Then, as now, my most deeply held commitments were clayfooted. I still stumble over them, longing for grace. So try as I did, there were misunderstandings over words and intentions. My best shots at a certain kind of relational integrity fell short of what would've made everyone flourish—and remembering that still makes me groan.

But what I began to learn then about the meaning of friendship still runs through my life. Friendship isn't second best. Human beings that we are, we are profoundly made for community. We are never ourselves fully, by ourselves. We cannot *not* be in relationship, honest and true relationships with men and woman with whom we work at the meaning of our common life. Humanity is a bi-unity for everyone everywhere; male and female we were created, and we were created for community.

In this wounded world, there are a thousand ways to be wounded. Disappointments of all kinds, deaths of every sort. But even when we find heartache rather than happiness, even when our experience of knowing and being known ends in tragic betrayal, we still long for friendships that matter. They keep our hearts alive, reminding us that sometimes some people can be trusted, that sometimes some people will be there, push come to horribly sad shove.

In those adolescent-becoming-adult years, what was seen very much through a glass darkly is now more clearly seen. People who like being married, who over time find honest happiness in marriage are most of all friends—good friends, true and trusted friends. Over time, marriage is not a long date. Instead it is a long friendship, a dear and unique friendship, a completely unique friendship.

When I began thinking more seriously about Meg, beginning to see that our friendship was different, that she was honestly unique to me, unlike any other woman I knew, there were several factors that made me want to marry her. She was pretty, she was kind, she cared about things that mattered most in life and learning. She was from a family with whom my family had a long history—and she made scrumptious cinnamon rolls! That she had hiked over the Continental Divide in Colorado, twenty miles from one side of Rocky Mountain National Park to the other in one day, sealed my heart.

Simply said, she loved what I loved—and a friend she was, a good friend I wanted to marry. In the ins and outs of life, being husband and wife now for most of life, we are still friends and still eating her delicious cinnamon rolls sometimes. And though we are no longer bounding over boulders as we once did, we are still hiking the trails of life together, still seeing and hearing the world, finding our place in it.

Photo of my wife, Meg, looking across the Atlantic from the cliffs of Columbkille in Donegal, Ireland.

ON MERE CHRISTIANITY

MOST OF MY LIFE AGO I decided that I would believe only things in my truest heart that honest Christians had believed in every century and every culture. That has been my hope, stumbling along as I do.

Good folk such as Richard Baxter and C. S. Lewis argued for this in their times, seeing a "central hallway" running through history—calling it "mere Christianity"—with the most important beliefs about God, the human condition, and history at the center of this long conversation among people of honest and historic faith. The Orthodox would have their door off the hallway, as would the Catholics, as would the Protestants—and within those doors would be smaller conversations, often debates, between the Russian Orthodox and the Greek Orthodox, between the Jesuits and the Benedictines, between Anglicans and Presbyterians, and on and on and on.

And sometimes those conversations matter very much, sometimes those debates are very important, and sometimes probably not so much. To know which is which is one of the most difficult tasks of the human heart.

Being on Inisheer Island, Ireland, for a few days reminded me of the deeper, longer truths of life and my life. The locals say that there are ten thousand miles of stone fences on the three Aran Islands; on Inisheer we counted five trees, which gives one pause, realizing that for a very long time people have carved out a life on these barren rocks, creating an agricultural economy from the stone, sand, and seaweed. Throughout the world, the wool from the Aran Island's sheep has made for some of the finest sweaters we know.

In this place where history and wonder meet, there is an ancient church from the tenth century, now sunken into the ground because of one thousand years of blowing sand, calling out to us through the generations, reminding us of the truest truths of the universe. For almost as long as we know, women and men have set their hope on the cross, seeing its reality as the center of life and learning, of labor and love.

While the details are hard to know so many years later, it is believed that St. Brendan went out from and returned to Inisheer in the sixth century, as did St. Columba about that same time. Their visionary vocations mattered then and still do centuries later, choosing to step into history not knowing where their adventures would take them, sure that they had been called to love the world in Christ's name. Inisheer Island—a simple place—is almost forgotten now, but for folk who see themselves as belonging to the deep, long story of the gospel of the kingdom, *mere Christianity*. It matters, its influence echoing across time into eternity. For hundreds of years men and women have lived there, with *ora et labora* at the heart of their hope, seeing the world for what it is and isn't, and choosing to step into it for love's sake.

Simply said, I have chosen that Story to make sense of my story—and therefore Inisheer Island has meaning for the person I am, for the person I want to be.

Photo of a Celtic cross in Inisheer Island, Ireland.

REMARKABLE JOY,
REMARKABLE SORROW

SOMETIMES WE READ something and it simply jumps off of the page. Most of twenty years ago I began reading *Reflecting the Glory*, the Lenten meditations of N. T. Wright, and these words caught my heart.

> We discover that the story of Jesus' ministry is not only the story of what he did in history, but encompasses also the vocation that comes to us in the present: that we should be, in the power of the Spirit, the presence of Jesus for the whole world. This discovery brings the most remarkable joy and the most remarkable sorrow. This is our vocation: to take up our cross, and be Jesus for the whole world, living with the joy and the sorrow woven into the pattern of our days.

Yes.

The world of Pixar's *Inside Out* gives us a window into the human heart, full of complexity it is, born of pushes and pulls from many different places, clamoring in their various ways for our attention.

Anger. Fear. Disgust. Sadness. Joy. There is more to us, human beings that we are, but *Inside Out* is a broad-brushstroke account of the way we see and why we see the way we see. And while all of the emotions are written into the story, sadness and joy dominate. For most of the film they are in tension with each other, Sadness, an appropriately blue character shaped like a tear, touching things she should not touch because her touches mar memories, changing them forever, and Joy irresistibly brightening her moments and days with happiness for all.

Almost always we want Sadness to stay away from anything and everything that might be affected by her "Puddleglumness," remembering the character from Narnia who saw every cup as half empty and worse. And on the other side, Joy brings joy, casting aside what should not be for what might be, for what could be.

There is drama, of course, and it all plays out in the mind and heart of the little girl, desperately trying to make a new home in a new city. But as Anger, Fear, and Disgust battle for her soul, Sadness and Joy finally save the day, surprisingly coming to understand that a healthy heart makes room for both "remarkable joy and remarkable sorrow." They are not the same, and they are both true.

Every one of us knows that. In our different ways of living our humanness "inside out"—internally wrestling with the glorious ruins that we are even as we show and tell to the wider world the invisible realities playing out deep inside—we feel stretched taut between happiness and heartache, between joy and sadness.

When I read Wright, finding something profoundly true in his words, I remember thinking that I needed reasons to believe that could make honest sense of my life. I knew true joy, I knew true sorrow, and they were not the same thing. And I knew that I was not going to be a Buddhist, requiring myself to extinguish myself, expecting that someday I would finally see that everything was the same and that there was no meaning to the joy or to the sorrow, that they were illusions and not really real, neither the joy nor the sorrow.

Instead, I entered into the richness of the incarnation in a way I had never imagined, seeing in its theological vision a way to live in the world. That has been true, and it is still true. Day by day I am torn apart by the reality of sadness, overwhelmed by the remarkable sorrow that is ours as human beings. There are days when I despair and cannot imagine going on. But then it is also true that the sun comes up, the flowers bloom, the lambs leap, my grandchildren jump into my arms, my wife still loves me, and I remember to remember that there is remarkable joy too. Both are woven into the pattern of my days.

The best art tells the truth about life, giving us ways to see and hear the truth about who we are, of what it means to be human. Pixar has, playfully as it must, told a tale that twines together the complexity of the human heart, reminding us that a good life, an honest life, a happy life, is one in which sadness and joy are together written into the very meaning of life—at least until all things are made right, at least until all the wounds are healed, at least until we all join Gandalf in his longing for the day when all that is good becomes true.

Image from *Inside Out*, directed by Pete Docter and (codirector) Ronnie Del Carmen (copyright: Pixar Animation Studios, Emeryville, CA, 2015).

THE SANGRE DE CRISTOS

I WAS BORN UNDER THE SANGRE DE CRISTOS, and I have always liked that.

But adding to that gift, I was born in Monte Vista, a small town in the San Luis Valley of Colorado, a little place at the end of a long highway so straight that it is called "the gun barrel"—with a mountain view of the grand peaks running along the Rio Grande as it makes its way from the headwaters in the Rockies down into New Mexico, and finally along the wide spaces that border Texas and Mexico, eventually emptying itself in the Gulf. For most of a hundred miles, fourteen thousand foot high mountains tower over the valley.

About three hundred years ago, a Spanish explorer made his way from Mexico into Colorado, following the Rio Grande, and the story that is told is that when he saw the sunrise and sunset over the peaks, he exclaimed, "Sangre de Cristo!" *The blood of Christ.*

In a more sacramental age—one more attentive to transcendence threading its way through the universe, one even born of Christian faith, sadly twined together as it too often was with military might and economic exploitation—that Antonio Valverde y Cosío named the mountains for the blood of Christ is understandable, even to our very secular ears. We've come a long way, sure as we are now that there are no windows to transcendence. "This is it . . . and this is all that ever has been and this is all that ever will be." There is nothing tinged with the sacred—not our mountains, our cities, our bodies, our hopes, or our dreams.

Being back in Colorado for the weekend, too short for a native like me, I thought about my life, about opening my eyes as a baby to the Sangre de Cristos, newly aware of the world, barely able to understand very much about it of course. But I did begin there, most of a lifetime ago. As I developed my lectures for the conference, speaking six times over three days, I decided to begin my thinking where I began. While I spoke on the themes from my *Visions of Vocation* book, as I spent days thinking it all through, it increasingly seemed clear to me that rooting myself in my roots made the most sense.

So throughout I talked about being the son of my father and the grandson of my grandfather, about their lives and labors, about the rhythms of days and weeks that made them *them*. Because I was asked to speak on "Worship to Workplace, and Back Again," I reflected on their visions of vocation, of who they were and what they did. From my father's work as a scientist tasked with the complexity of agricultural production in the San Luis Valley, focused specially on sheep and potatoes, to my grandfather's long work buying and selling cattle throughout Colorado, for years driving through the northern end of the San Luis Valley on his way over Wolf Creek Pass to Durango and Cortez. I talked about the different ways they were marked by *ora et labora*, that sense of seamlessness that became a fabric over a lifetime, weaving together prayer and work, day after day, year after year. Everything about them that matters most was born of the gift of long-loved loves, their marriage lasting for sixty years. That reality made them *them*, as it has made me *me*.

Wounded people that we are, living in a wounded world as we do, no one does this perfectly. We all stumble, and at our best we are signposts of what might be, of what could be, maybe even of what should be. Most of the time for most of us, we settle into the brokenness of life, choosing fragmentation, a dualism between what we long for in our truest longings and the way we live. So we compartmentalize, choosing to see some things as more important than others—sex, money, and freedom, for example—making them more important than they can ever possibly be. The ancients called this idolatry, and it still is. Born of our unwillingness to see seamlessly—to see everything as sacred, everything as born with meaning and purpose and yet and yet, broken, terribly and tragically broken, because we are—we live our lives as lies.

In the Christian vision of reality, of what it means to be human living in this world, the deepest hope is that someday what is broken will be made whole, that all the sorrows and sadness will be finally healed. Our hope is for more than "heaven," but for a cosmos renewed, a new heaven and a new earth, a promise born of the conviction that a final redemption will happen, that a reconciliation of all things will someday become what everyone will see and hear, that every knee will someday bow to this truth brought about by the blood of Christ. In theological terms, this is called atonement, an *at-one-ment*, where all things will finally and fully be as they were meant to be.

Hindus and Buddhists don't see it this way, nor do evolutionary materialists, each in their own unique ways arguing for "enlightenment," which is a strange and mysterious longing in every heart. We do want to know, we do want to see things as they really are, but in our broken hearts we choose lesser truths—for example, believing that sex and money and freedom can be more important than they ever finally can be. True, but not that true

There are lesser hopes for this eschatological satisfaction in the Jewish and Muslim traditions, yearning as they do for a final realization of what they believe about the world and their place in it. None of these hopes are despised, none are disdained. But there is something different and distinct about the story the Scriptures teach about the history from creation to consummation, of the world that was as it ought to be and the world that someday will be—and therefore the meaning of *sangre de Cristo* and its implications for all of life, for all of history, for all things in heaven and on earth.

So while at my best I see through a glass darkly, understanding some things a little bit and missing much more, most of my life later I am still glad to have been born under the Sangre de Cristos, certain that atonement has happened and that someday its promise will become reality. We live in a now-but-not-yet world. That has consequences for everything—for life and love, for labor and learning—brought together through a liturgical coherence that makes worship and workplace integrally connected, longing as we do for a time and place when and where *ora et labora* is who we are and how we live.

Photo of the Sangre de Cristos along the eastern edge of the San Luis Valley. Most of the one hundred miles of fourteen thousand foot peaks runs from Colorado into New Mexico.

UNCOMMON GRACE, UNCOMMON HEROISM

FOR A FEW YEARS I lived my life in light of the mountain men, imagining my very ordinary days enlarged by the companionship of Kit Carson, William Sublette, Jim Beckworth, Jedediah Smith, and Jim Bridger. Their adventures became my adventures.

I've long been a lover of stories and these tales told of brave men, unusual men, visionary men carving lives out of the rugged mountains of the American West. Trailblazers across the grand prairies, following the great rivers into the majestic Rockies, they lived among the native peoples, trapping beaver, rarely stopping for long as there was always one more mountain pass to discover.

In the little library that served our town, I read every biography of these men I could find and did the same in our school library. I didn't ponder the books, I swallowed them. And then the day came when I wasn't a boy anymore, and the books I read began to change. But years later I still look back on that time as wonderfully satisfying, remembering my hours and days spent alongside these heroes whose lives fueled my imagination.

Of course, I thought of all this while watching *The Revenant*, the film that sort of tells the tale of Hugh Glass, a mountain man best known for having met his match with an angry mama grizzly bear. We only have the broad brushstrokes of Glass's life, and so the screenwriters for the film have imagined a lot—the story is set in places that look like the American West, but they had to film in Alberta, British Columbia, and Argentina to get the mountains and skies and snow they wanted.

The actual story that has been passed down has a grace at its heart that is missed in the movie. No son was murdered, though there was a betrayal among companions, and when Glass finally found his betrayers, he forgave them—rather than, as the film offers, setting out into the snow to exact his revenge on the man who murdered his son. I suppose, in our coldhearted hearts, we are more drawn to bloodlust of every kind and expect an "eye for an eye" in life and on screen. Something murderous and hideous seems to go with our popcorn these days. To have an uncommon grace be the surprising climax would be a different story than we usually tell in our cineplex world. We want our blood and guts and hate and revenge, and *The Revenant* satisfies every one of those desires.

It is not that the film is without tenderness and humanity. The story told of Glass and his son, untrue to history as it is, is profoundly moving. Fathers love their sons in ways that sons almost never understand, and sons love their fathers with bonds that only blood can create; this is true more often than not, with tragic exceptions that are always heartaching. And the courageous rescue of the Arikara Indian woman by Glass, an important thread through the story, and her silent but sure protection of him at a moment when he could only see his death are heroic windows into the human heart.

But even with the grace that allowed him to keep his scalp, we are left with the exhaustion wrought by Glass's revenge. He did kill the one he wanted to kill, but for asking my attention for two and a half hours, I wanted more than a stab for a stab—as did Glass, if I read his face on the movie screen rightly. He got what he wanted but didn't find what he was looking for.

I hate cheap stories and cheap endings, so I am not looking for Pollyanna. Instead, I long for movies that wrestle with the complexity of the human condition, ones that remember to weave both glory and ruin into the fabric of a film. In the reality of life for every son of Adam and daughter of Eve, grace is the most difficult of all choices, even harder than fighting for your life across the wintry cold of the Wild West. To turn the other cheek requires more from us than any other decision, which is why we so rarely forgive—and why revenge is always easier and therefore is always a cheaper ending to a story.

I confess that reading about the true Glass, and finding that he gave grace, made him more heroic. The film *The Revenant* almost requires revenge, but I wonder: If the moral imagination had been different, would the storytellers have given us a film for the ages, a story to be told again and again, generation after generation?

A good story about a good person is hard to tell, but it is a story we all long to hear.

Image from *The Revenant*, directed by Alejandro G. Iñárritu (copyright: Twentieth Century Fox, Los Angeles, 2015).

WHO ARE WE AND WHY
DOES IT MATTER?

"PUTTING IT TO BED." In the world I once lived in, that was how we talked about getting the magazine out the door, ready for printing.

Flying over the San Francisco Bay, I saw part of the Dumbarton Bridge running across the water from the west side of the bay to the east side, and I recalled that season of my young life. For a year I lived in Palo Alto, having dropped out of college with questions to ask that college couldn't answer. And yes, I lived in a commune—frail, finite people that we were. Together we worked on a magazine called *Renaissance*, "a radically Christian critique of culture." My job was as managing editor, and so most of what I did was create the look, order the articles and edit them, lay it out, and get it to the printer.

As a twenty-year-old, I was pretty intimidated by the older ones in our little community and just couldn't imagine that I had anything to say that anyone would want to read. But I had more experience than most at the managing editor things, so that was my task. As each issue was finally ready, often in the wee hours of the night, I would drive across the bay to the large printing company we had contracted with and give them my work.

Those were pretty heady days, the "countercultural revolution" we called them. Everything seemed possible, even though everything was horribly marred at the very same time. We took that on, issue by issue, writing articles about films and filmmakers, plays and playwrights, authors and their books, trying to understand what it all meant. Glorious ruins we are as human beings, that year I began to see into the meaning of it all for the first time. What we believed about human nature, about the human condition, affected everything else—life and love, politics and economics, sex and money, the arts of every kind, work for everyone everywhere.

I hitchhiked a lot that year, almost weekly going across the bay to Berkeley, sitting in on conversations with gurus representing a universe of worlds and worldviews, all the while sifting and sorting through my own beliefs about everything.

In many ways, that year was a year along the way for me, one where I read a lot, listened a lot, and asked a lot of questions. As the months passed I was increasingly sure that I wanted to take my new backpack (purchased that year at a little company making their own stuff, selling it out of a converted garage in Berkeley—calling themselves "North Face" after the mountainside in Yosemite) and hitchhike my way to Europe.

So I traveled from California to New York, thumb to the road, and got on an Icelandic Airlines flight to Europe (as all pilgrims did, I think), making my way across the British Isles and eventually to Switzerland.

I was going to L'Abri, a small place in the world, with different windows into its promise that one could ask honest questions and get honest answers. In the most desperate way, driven by the deepest hopes, I wanted that. I needed that.

Years later, most of my life later, I am sure that others do too. We are like that as human beings. We have things we think about, things we care about, and apart from suppressing them into the darkest places of our hearts, we will find ways to make sense of them. Having been formed by those years, I have spent my life opening myself to people like I was, inviting them into a way of learning that takes questions seriously and takes answers seriously too, sure that being honest about who we are as human beings is the thread to follow, if we are going to find our way . . . because we will get lost otherwise.

Photo of the Golden Gate Bridge in San Francisco, California.

WHOLE HEARTS,
BROKEN HEARTS

For many years I have read and reread versions of the story
of the prodigal son during the days of Lenten meditation. There
are good books written about it, such as Henri Nouwen's *The
Return of the Prodigal*, and wise reflections on it from people such

as Helmut Thielicke in *The Waiting Father*. But there are other stories too, perhaps the most wonderful of all stories, *Les Misérables* by Victor Hugo. And more recently in the late twentieth century, Susan Howatch has given us *Glittering Images*, which is its own imaginative account of a man stumbling along, longing for grace.

Most recently it was Michael O'Brien's *The Father's Tale*. If there is one image that runs its way through, it is this: the only whole heart is a broken heart. A hard truth, but a truth worth pondering in every season of every year.

O'Brien sets this story in the very contemporary world of a twenty-first century Canadian bookseller whose wife has died. He is also the father of two sons, prodigal in their different ways. As must be, they weigh on his heart because they are his heart, flesh of his own flesh.

While the father becomes consumed with the health, body, and soul of one of his sons, lost in unimaginable ways, following after him to Oxford, London, Helsinki, St. Petersburg, Moscow, and finally to the outer regions of Russia and the wilds of Siberia, the story is mostly, and not surprisingly, a story of the father's own heart. Broken as it is, for many reasons in many ways, his journey is a pilgrimage toward a whole heart.

There is nothing cheap here. The very best and the very worst are offered, the hopes and fears of every one of us, with great satisfactions and horrible sorrows. They ring true to the world that is ours; we know this story because it is our story.

How do we find our way to whole hearts? I have yet to discover a good map, a way set out that connects the dots, one by one, with three easy steps. There is in me, quite deeply, a resistance to being broken, and more and more broken. I want to be well; in the deepest possible way, I want to be well. I long for the hurts and the wounds to be finally and fully healed. There is nothing I want more than that. The strains that are ours as individuals, the sorrows that each family knows, the burdens born by communities, the distorted desires of nations; in ways we know and don't know, the brokenness is everywhere, from our most personal relationships to our most public responsibilities.

The longing of every heart, and of my heart, is so intense. We want the tears to be gone, the aches to be over. While it is still mysterious to me, through a glass darkly as it is, I think I understand a bit more of the relationship between a whole heart and a broken heart—and I sigh, torn as I am between what I am and what I want to be. Knowing that the way to one is the other is the hard truth, the strange grace, of *The Father's Tale*, but like the best stories always are, it is a story for all of us.

At our home in Virginia we have sixteen dogwood trees of different varieties and I love each one. In the spring they offer their delicately imagined flowers that tell, as tradition says, of the Passion of Christ.

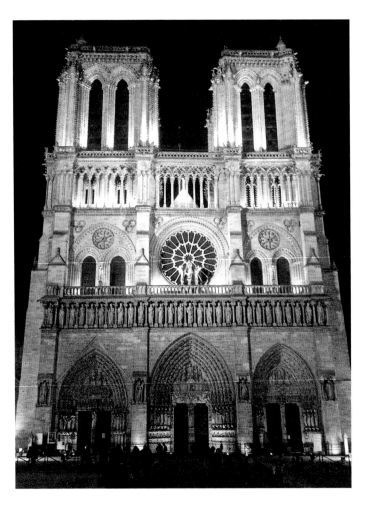

AN ENDING

AS WE HAVE FOR MANY YEARS, we had our neighbors with us for the Fourth of July, bringing our summery foods for a common meal, talking into the evening about a million things.

Before it was over, two of my long friends mentioned in the course of our conversation, "Proximate, yes?" And I smiled, knowing what they meant. We were talking about life and the world, near and far; our families, our work, the questions of our life together as Americans and as citizens of a globalizing planet. And because we know each other well, we know the way we see and hear the world around us.

Proximate is a good word for us. In our different ways we all long for the world to be made right. We all long for justice and mercy to be done on the face of the earth. We all long for what is real and true and right to be woven into the fabric of our flourishing as citizens of our cities and societies. The work of our days reflects those commitments, each of us living the hope that is ours in common, doing our best in the vocations that thread through our lives to be common grace for the common good.

But each of us finds it very hard. In different ways we all experience the pains and sorrows of work that is less than what we expect, at least less than what it seems it ought to be. Unpopular causes are just that. Difficult and complex ideas are hard to understand. The twistedness of the human heart makes everything we know and love *less than* it could be and should be.

Some of the challenges we talked about are the most intractable ones we know, and the world, the flesh, and the devil conspire against what good might be done. What Iris Murdock called "the fat relentless ego" winds its way through even our best efforts—it is hard enough to control our own selves, much less the selves of others. To choose for a true common good is almost impossible, given who we are.

As we made our way through the evening, "Proximate, yes?" came up several times. The word has become one that matters to us because we are people who—while longing for what is to be what should be, for the wounds of life and the world to be finally and fully healed—know that in this frail, fallen life, that is not going to happen tomorrow. And it might not even happen this year.

What do we do then?

It is always possible to give up, knowing that we tried, and it just didn't work. We gave our best shots, and we lost. But it is within the dynamic of hope hoped for that we have come to the word *proximate*. Can we try, and try again, making peace with something, even if it is not everything?

I know that this is one of the hardest questions of my life. In my deepest being I want everything in my life and in the wide world to be made right. I can hardly stand it that this doesn't happen. Enough of "less than"! But living the life I have, I know that those who sustain their commitments and loves are people who make peace with the proximate. Whether that is in marriage, in the most personal of all the relationships we know, or whether that is in the public square, in the most political of the responsibilities that are ours. We have no other life, and we have no other world.

Because this is true, I think about the challenge of the proximate almost all the time.

This past spring I was surprised to find that Victor Hugo did too. During the days of Lent, I was pondering his lesser-known novel, the story of the hunchback of Notre Dame. For years I had read in

Les Miserables during my Lenten meditations, especially the story "The Just Man," which tells the tale of the bishop over most of a hundred pages. Who was he? Why was he? What made him respond to Jean Valjean as he did? And knowing that I knew less about the hunchback, I thought that I would learn more about this man who was so notably broken, as that reality is the one I want to ponder during Lent.

What I discovered is that his name, Quasimodo, comes from the Latin liturgy, and is what the church has called the Sunday following Easter, naming it "low Sunday" (*quasi modo*)—not quite the glory of Easter, but now back into ordinary time and life. We have to make peace with something that is real and true and right, even if it is not the "everything" of Easter. As the deformed foundling was found on that day, Hugo writes, "He wanted the name to typify just how incomplete and half-finished the poor little creature was. And in fact, Quasimodo, one-eyed, hunchbacked and crook-kneed, was hardly more than an 'approximation.'"

These words of Hugo jumped off the page. Very literally, the etymology of the word means "as if, as though, in approximation, somewhat like, not far from" what we have expected. Yes, less than.

While the hunchback's story is not mine for a thousand reasons, it is mine in a more profound way. On some level, in some way, I wanted to ponder my own incompleteness, my own frailty, as hard as that is. While it is a great challenge to honestly address the heartaches of the world, it is even a greater challenge to see ourselves honestly, to own up to our own ways of falling short of the glory of God, even of our own expectations of what we ought to be. In a word, to see that at our best we "approximate" what a good life means.

At the word *proximate* I smiled, knowing what it means and why it matters. We cannot keep going if we don't have a word like that. Even a great novelist like Hugo understood this. If we are serious about keeping our hearts alive over time, we have to make peace with the proximate, knowing the wounds of the world will become too much, knowing that our own wounds are too much. Something is something—because it is not nothing, even if it is not everything.

Photo from a nighttime stroll along the Seine several years ago, seeing the grandeur of the Cathedral of Notre Dame, and yes, wondering about its bells, and the hunchback who tolled them.

ACKNOWLEDGMENTS

Dᴏsᴛᴏᴇᴠᴋsʏ ᴏɴᴄᴇ ᴏʙsᴇʀᴠᴇᴅ ᴛʜᴀᴛ "the best definition of man is the ungrateful biped." Tragically, I am, and we are, too often.

But wanting more than that, hoping for a more honest heart, I know that this book has been born over years as the gift of friends who know me well enough to know what I think about, and what I write about—and sometimes even what I see as I see the world through the lens of my camera. And they have urged me to bring together essays with photos, offering them for a wider reading. So now I have.

First among friends is the great friend of my life, my wife, Meg, my long-loved love. Thank you for reading, and reading again, listening to the questions that have become these essays—and for your grace in looking at the world through the lenses of my life. The honest grace you give has sustained me, kept me at the life together that is ours, with gladness and singleness of heart.

We have lived our life by the credo of the Clapham community of two hundred years ago, a group of differently gifted people working together over a generation for the renewal of their society, who believed that one should "chose a neighbor before one chooses a house." That has been our commitment through the years, across America and now into Canada. This book was born among a community of dear friends in Virginia, folks like us who also were called into the capital city of Washington, DC. Through thick and thin over more than twenty-five years, from every kind of happiness to every kind of heartache, from having babies ourselves to seeing our babies have their own babies, from the sharing of birthdays and holidays year after year, from entering into the depth and range of our common loves and labors, we have known the joys and sorrows of life together, laughing and weeping across time. Your stories are told throughout this book, and while thank you seems small, it is true.

These friends are among a community of men and women whose care has kept me going at critical moments, knowing that I needed the gift of a good word. I think of Andi Ashworth and Charlie Peacock, Byron Borger, Beau Boulter, Ray and B.J. Blunt, Michael Bontrager, Brett Bradshaw, Bob Burns, Scott Calgaro, Uli Chi, Milan Cicel, Morna Comeau, Jeff Crosby, Todd and Judi Deatherage, Susan Den Herder, Al Erisman, Bill Fullilove, Brad Frey, Rich Gathro, Brad Gibson, Don Guthrie, Jeff Greenman, Denis and Margie Haack, Kate Harris, Jon Hart, Jerry Herbert, Hans Hess, Shirley Hoogstra, Jay Jakub, Matt Kaemingk, David Kiersznowski, Kwang Kim, John Kyle, Drew Masterson, Phil Mollenkof, Steve Moore, Jim Mullins, Jena Lee Nardella, Tom Nelson, Peter Ochs, J. I. Packer, John Penrose, Madison Perry, Allan Poole, Clydette Powell, Russ Pulliam, Steven Purcell, Brad Reeves, Mark Roberts, Mark and Leanne Rodgers, Gustavo Santos, Shauna Schneider, Steve Skancke, Fred Smith, Paul Stevens, Lisa Park Slayton, John Terrill, Adam Theis, David Turner, Walt Turner, Rick Wellock, Todd Wahrenberger, Suby Wildman, John Yates, and Nancy Ziegler. Thank you each one.

And finally, this book would not be a book without the editorial wisdom of Elissa Schauer and Cindy Bunch, colleagues as we have been and friends that we are.